Tree Cover and Aridity Projections to 2060

A Technical Document Supporting the Forest Service 2010 RPA Assessment

Eric J. Greenfield and David J. Nowak

Abstract

Future projections of tree cover and climate change are useful to natural resource managers from the local to national level as they illustrate potential changes to our natural resources and the ecosystem services they provide. By understanding these potential changes, management strategies can be set to sustain desired levels of healthy natural resources for future generations. In support of the 2010 Renewable Resources Planning Act (RPA) Assessment, this report a) details three projections of tree cover change across the conterminous United States based on predicted land-use changes from 2000 to 2060; b) evaluates nine climate projections for the same period to assess which areas of the country may become more or less arid; and c) provides an index of combined tree-cover and aridity change for nine modeled projections to illustrate which areas of the United States are projected to experience the greatest impact from tree-cover loss and increasing aridity. The index illustrates a new approach to highlight areas of ecological vulnerability or concern that may develop at the nexus of projected land use and climate change. We found that in all projections the conterminous United States loses tree cover by 2060, ranging from a 1.1 to 1.6 percent decline; and that the conterminous United States is becoming more arid by 2060, ranging from a 0.05 to 0.19 decrease in the aridity ratio. Overall, the frequency and magnitude of percent tree cover losses and aridity increases among the counties of the conterminous United States are greater than percent tree cover gains and decreases in aridity. The index illustrates that the areas at greatest risk of ecological change from tree loss and increased aridity generally are rapidly urbanizing regions of high tree cover and low aridity such as those found in the metropolitan regions of the Pacific Northwest, Southeast, and Northeast.

Authors

ERIC J. GREENFIELD is a forester with the U.S. Forest Service's Northern Research Station at Syracuse, New York.

DAVID J. NOWAK is a research forester and project leader with the U.S. Forest Service's Northern Research Station at Syracuse, New York.

Manuscript received for publication January 2013

Published by:

USDA FOREST SERVICE
11 CAMPUS BLVD., SUITE 200
NEWTOWN SQUARE, PA 19073-3294

October 2013

For additional copies:

USDA Forest Service
Publications Distribution
359 Main Road
Delaware, OH 43015-8640
Fax: 740-368-0152

Visit our homepage at: **http://www.nrs.fs.fed.us/**

Tree Cover and Aridity Projections to 2060: A Technical Document Supporting the Forest Service 2010 RPA Assessment

Eric J. Greenfield

David J. Nowak

CONTENTS

LIST OF TABLES

LIST OF FIGURES

ACKNOWLEDGMENTS

Funding for this project was provided, in part, by the U.S. Forest Service's RPA Assessment Staff and State & Private Forestry's Urban and Community Forestry Program.

The authors would also like to thank and acknowledge the following: Linda L. Langner, RPA Assessment National Program Leader at the U.S. Forest Service's Research and Development Washington Office for her coordination, review, and editing; and David P. Coulson, Linda A. Joyce, and David N. Wear for their review of the original manuscript.

Tree Cover and Aridity Projections to 2060: A Technical Document Supporting the Forest Service 2010 RPA Assessment

Eric J. Greenfield

David J. Nowak

INTRODUCTION

Forests are an essential component of America's "green infrastructure" and trees play particularly important roles in providing ecosystem services and enhancing human health. Trees provide various ecosystem services such as improvements in air and water quality, building energy conservation, cooler air temperatures, reductions in ultraviolet radiation, and many other environmental, economic and social benefits (e.g., Kuo and Sullivan 2001, Nowak and Dwyer 2007, Ulrich 1984, Westphal 2003, Wolf 2003). Costs associated with trees can be economic (e.g., planting and maintenance, increased building energy costs), social (obstructed views, litter, storm debris), and environmental (e.g., pollen, volatile organic compound emissions) (Nowak and Dwyer 2007). In addition, there can be transaction costs associated with the necessary institutional arrangements (setting, communicating, adapting policy) that aid forest management (Hardy and Koontz 2010, Ostrom 1990).

This report provides supporting documentation to the Forest Service 2010 Resources Planning Act (RPA) Assessment, Future of America's Forests and Rangelands (U.S. Forest Service 2012a). The 2010 RPA Assessment, the fifth report prepared in response to the mandate in the Forest and Rangeland Renewable Resources Planning Act (RPA 1974), summarizes findings about the status, trends, and projected future of forests, rangelands, wildlife and fish, biodiversity, water, outdoor recreation, wilderness, and urban

forests, and the effects of climate change upon these resources. The RPA Assessment provides information to resource managers and policymakers from the national down to the local scale so they can develop strategies to sustain natural resources into the future. The key findings from the assessment document are a) land development will continue to threaten the integrity of natural ecosystems; b) climate change will alter natural ecosystems and affect their ability to provide goods and services; c) competition for goods and services from natural ecosystems will increase; and d) geographic variation in resource responses to drivers of change will require regional and local strategies to address resource management issues.

The future tree cover in the United States will change with the changes in land uses and climates outlined within the RPA Assessment, affecting the amount of benefits derived from this resource and the costs associated with managing or maintaining forests. This report details three projections of tree cover change across the conterminous United States based on predicted land-use changes from 2000 to 2060. It also evaluates nine climate projections for the same period to assess which areas of the country may become more or less arid. Finally this report provides an index of combined tree-cover and aridity change for nine modeled projections to illustrate which areas of the United States are projected to experience the greatest impact from tree-cover loss and increasing aridity. The index illustrates a new approach to highlight areas of ecological vulnerability or concern that may develop at the nexus of projected land use and climate change. We found that in all projections, the conterminous United States loses tree cover by 2060, ranging from a 1.1 to 1.6 percent decline; and that the conterminous United States is becoming more arid by 2060, ranging from a 0.05 to 0.19 decrease in the aridity ratio. Overall, the frequency and magnitude of percent tree cover losses and aridity increases among the counties of the conterminous United States are greater than percent tree cover gains and decreases in aridity. The index illustrates that the areas at greatest risk of ecological change from tree loss and increased

aridity generally are rapidly urbanizing regions of high tree cover and low aridity such as those found in the metropolitan regions of the Pacific Northwest, Southeast, and Northeast (Fig. 1).

2010 RPA Scenarios

The RPA Assessment addresses a wide range of economic and ecological phenomena. Because there are uncertainties about future political, economic, social, and environmental change, we used scenarios to explore a range of possible futures for U.S. renewable natural resources. The projection period was 2010 to 2060.

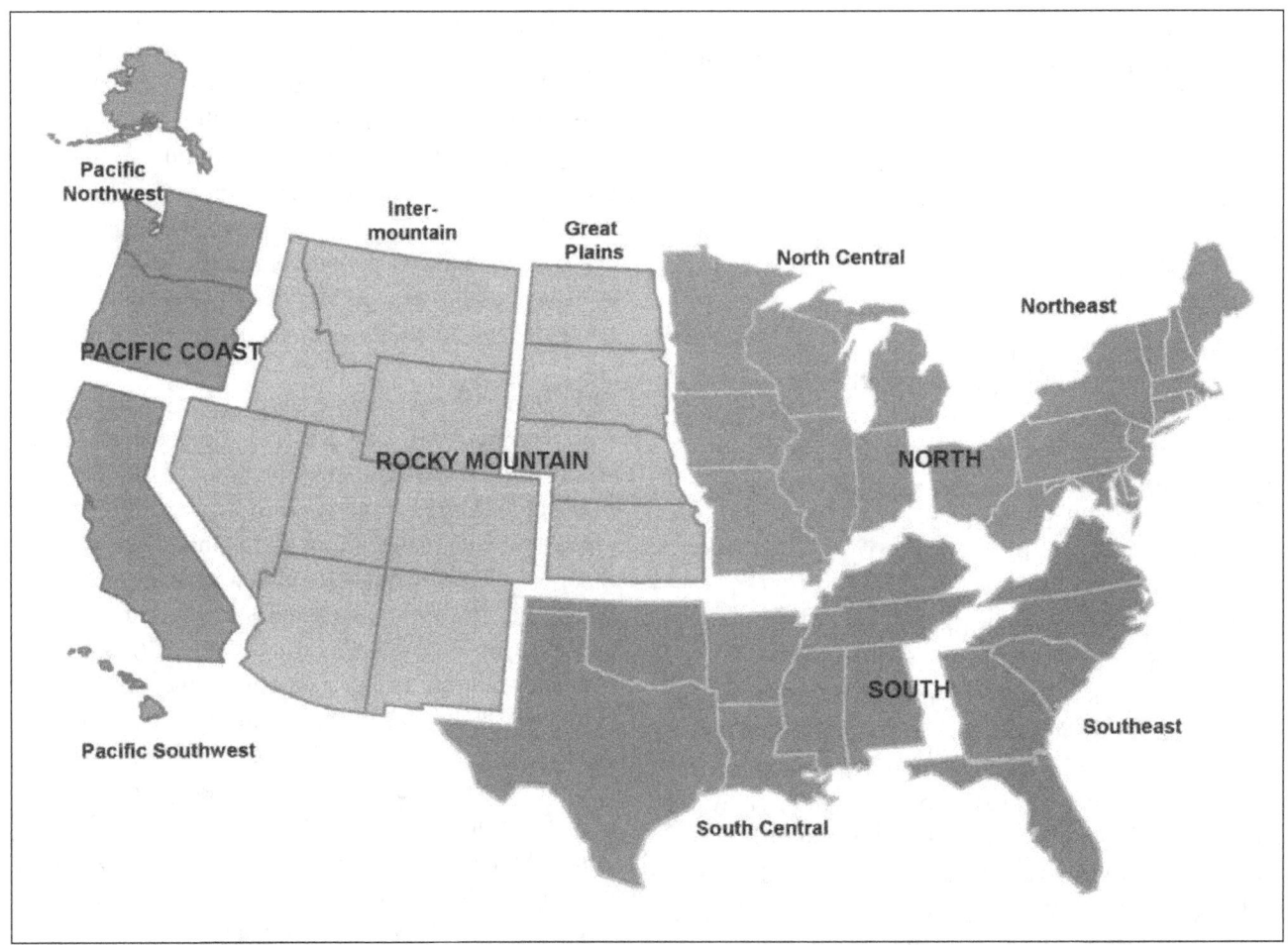

Figure 1.—RPA assessment regions of the United States

Three scenarios[1] were used to characterize common demographic, socioeconomic, and technological driving forces that underlay changes in resource conditions and to evaluate the sensitivity of resource trends to a feasible future range of these driving forces. These three RPA scenarios (Table 1) were linked to global scenarios developed for the Intergovernmental Panel on Climate Change (IPCC) Third Assessment Report (TAR) and Fourth Assessment Report (AR4) through IPCC assumptions and projections of global population growth, economic growth, bioenergy use, and climate (IPCC 2007). For continuity, we retained the scenario designations used in the IPCC TAR and AR4, with the addition of "RPA" to remind readers that these scenarios are tied to IPCC assumptions described in the Special Report on Emission Scenarios (SRES) (Nakicenovic and Swart 2000), but that some adjustments were made that are described in U.S. Forest Service (2012b). The RPA scenarios are therefore designated as RPA A1B, RPA A2, and RPA B2. Multiple climate projections were made for each IPCC scenario. The climate projections vary across scenarios in response to the associated levels of

greenhouse gas (GHG) emissions, but they also vary within a scenario because general circulation models (GCMs) differ in their approaches to modeling climate dynamics. Therefore, we selected climate projections from three GCMs for each of the three RPA scenarios to capture a range of future climates. Table 2 lists the IPCC scenarios and associated GCM projections that were used to develop climate projections for the RPA scenarios.

Land use change was projected by Wear (2011) for all counties in the conterminous United States for five major Natural Resource Inventory (NRI) land use classes: forest land, cropland, rangeland, urban and built-up areas, and pastureland and native pasture. Wear developed three land use distribution forecasts based on the three RPA scenarios using econometric models fit to historical data to allocate rural land among competing uses that incorporate projected changes in population and income at the county scale. Details of the methods and results can be found in Wear (2011). All land use change was assumed to occur on nonfederal land within these NRI categories; all other uses are held constant during the projection period, including Federal land, water area, enrolled Conservation Reserve Program lands, and utility corridors. The land use projections do not assume any

---

[1] A fourth scenario was developed to address variation in future bioenergy use, but that scenario was not used for the analysis described in this document.

Table 1.—Key characteristics of the RPA scenarios[a]

Characteristic	Scenario RPA A1B	Scenario A2	Scenario B2
IPCC general global description	Globalization, economic convergence	Regionalism, less trade	Slow change, localized solutions
IPCC global real GDP growth 2010-2060	High (6.2X)	Low (3.2X)	Medium (3.5X)
IPCC global population growth 2010-2060	Medium (1.3X)	High (1.7X)	Medium (1.4X)
IPCC global expansion of primary biomass energy production	High	Medium	Medium
U.S. GDP growth 2006-2060	Medium (3.3X)	Low (2.6X)	Low (2.2X)
U.S. population growth 2006-2060	Medium (1.5X)	High (1.7X)	Low (1.3X)

[a] Numbers in parenthesis are the factors of change in the projection period. For example, U.S. GDP increases by a factor of 3.3 times between 2010 and 2060 for scenario A1B.
GDP = gross domestic product.
IPCC = Intergovernmental Panel on Climate Change

Table 2.—IPCC scenarios and GCMs used for the 2010 RPA Assessment climate projections[a]

Scenario	GCM	Model vintage
A1B, A2	CGCM3.1(T47) (Canadian Centre for Climate Modeling and Analysis Third Generation Coupled Global Climate Model Version 3.1	AR4
	MIROC3.2(medres) (Australian Commonwealth Scientific and Industrial Research Organisation Mk 3.5 Climate System Model)	
	CSIRO-Mk3.5 (Japanese Centre for Climate System Research, University of Tokyo, National Institute for Environmental Studies and Frontier Research Center for Global Change Model for Interdisciplinary Research on Climate Version 3.2)	
B2	CGCM2 (Second Generation Coupled Global Climate Model)	TAR
	CSIRO-Mk2 (Mk 2 Climate System Model)	
	UKMO-HadCM3 (Hadley Centre for Climate Prediction and Research, UK)	

[a] AR4 climate projections were downloaded from the web portal for the World Climate Research Program Coupled Model Intercomparison Project phase 3, and TAR climate projections were downloaded from the IPCC Data Distribution Centre. See Joyce et al. (in review) for details on the climate data and the downscaling procedures used.
IPCC=Intergovernmental Panel on Climate Change
GCM=general circulation model

significant change in land use policy or regulations, i.e., projections are policy-neutral, based on historical land use relationships driven by future population and economic growth assumptions. The forecasted land uses are not influenced by climate.

In all RPA scenarios, increased urban and developed use is the dominant force in land use change, and all other land uses are projected to lose area. Urban and developed area increases the most in scenario RPA A1B, almost doubling the amount of urban area between 2010 and 2060. Forest land declines the most across the other land uses, with more than 30 million acres projected to be lost in RPA A1B. The largest forest land declines occur in the South, reflecting both an abundant forest resource and the highest projected population growth and urbanization (U.S. Forest Service 2012a).

METHODS

Three types of analyses were conducted to understand the possible effects of changes in land use and climate on tree cover: a) projected change in percent tree cover from 2000 to 2060; b) projected change in aridity from 2000 to 2060; and c) combined index of

change in percent tree cover and aridity from 2000 to 2060.

Tree Cover Projections

Tree cover projections in 2060 were derived by applying base year (2000) percent tree cover by land cover classes to projected land use changes. The model assumes that these land cover percent tree cover values will remain constant within their respective land uses over time. The data for this model comes from 2001 National Land Cover Database (NLCD) land cover and adjusted tree-cover data (Nowak and Greenfield 2010, USGS 2008), and models of projected land uses under the three future RPA scenarios A1B, A2, and B2 for the conterminous United States from 1997 to 2060 described previously (Wear 2011). For this analysis, both 2001 values from the NLCD and 1997 values from Wear (2011) were designated as the base year 2000. Adjusted NLCD tree cover values were used because original tree-cover estimates from the NLCD underestimated percent tree cover compared with photo-interpreted estimates (Nowak and Greenfield 2010). NLCD percent tree cover was modified according to the Nowak and Greenfield (2010) photo-interpreted values categorized by generalized

NLCD land cover classes within individual mapping zones.

The NRI land use classes used by Wear (2011) and the NLCD land cover categories are similar, but do not exactly match. The two sets of classes were reconciled with each other as follows (Table 3). The NLCD classes of developed land were associated with the NRI urban and built-up land category. The NLCD forested land cover classes were related with the NRI forest land category. The NLCD classes for agriculture were summed and associated with a summed agriculture category calculated from NRI cropland, and pastureland and native pasture categories. All other NLCD classes and NRI categories were related together as an "other" category to allow 100 percent distribution within each county. From these data, the proportion of each county land area within the combined categories of developed/urban, forest, agriculture, and other was calculated for the years 2000 and 2060. The adjusted average percent tree cover by NLCD land cover class was extracted by county and applied to the 2000 land use distribution in the county. The 2060 percent tree cover in each county was then calculated by weighting county-specific land use tree cover values by 2060 land use area. Tree-cover changes from 2000 to 2060 were projected for each of the three RPA scenarios: A1B, A2, and B2. Changes in percent tree cover were calculated as county percent tree cover in 2060 minus county percent tree cover in 2000.

Aridity Projections

Aridity is a climate attribute that describes the amount of dryness of a region. Aridity influences ecosystem properties of a region, and changes in aridity may indicate areas of concern for ecosystem change. The aridity index used in this analysis utilizes precipitation and potential evapotranspiration data from Coulson et al. (2010a and 2010b). Changes in aridity were projected from 2000 to 2060 using the three RPA scenarios (A1B, A2, B2), each having climate projections based on different models (Coulson et al. 2010a, 2010b; Joyce et al. in review) (Table 2). The base year 2000 climate estimate used in this analysis was derived from the historical climate data found in Coulson and Joyce (2010). These climate models contain the following data downscaled to the counties of the conterminous United States:

- Monthly totals of precipitation (mm)
- Monthly means of maximum and minimum daily temperatures (°C)
- Monthly mean of daily potential evapotranspiration (mm)

To provide decadal projections beginning in 2000, the individual county climate data were summarized into mean annual values based on decadal averages summed from monthly to annual values (e.g., average annual climate data for 2000 was based on average values from 1995 to 2004 inclusive, and 2060 was based on average values from 2055 to 2064 inclusive). Based on the climatic averages, an aridity index was calculated as the ratio of precipitation (P) to potential evapotranspiration (PE) (i.e., P/PE). In this dataset, potential evapotranspiration is calculated from temperature, elevation, dew point, and latitude variables (Coulson et al. 2010a, 2010b; Coulson and Joyce 2010). Aridity values were summarized within

Table 3.—Reconciling NRI and NLCD land use/cover classes

Analysis Categories	NRI Categories	NLCD Categories
Forest	Forest land	Deciduous forest, evergreen forest, mixed forest
Agriculture	Cropland, pastureland and native pasture	Cultivated crops, pasture/hay
Developed/urban	Urban and built-up areas	Developed-open space, developed-low intensity, developed-medium intensity, developed-high intensity

the following categories (Middleton and Thomas 1997):

- Hyperarid (P/PE < 0.05)
- Arid (0.05 to < 0.2)
- Semi-arid (0.2 to < 0.5)
- Dry subhumid (0.5 to < 0.65)
- Humid (P/PE > 0.65)

For the purposes of clearer illustration in this report and in the figures, changes in aridity from 2000 to 2060 by county were calculated as county aridity index (P/PE) in 2000 minus aridity index in 2060, so that increasing aridity is indicated by positive values. Likewise, a decrease in the aridity ratio means an increase in aridity.

Aridity and Tree Cover Change Index 2000 to 2060

The purpose of a combined aridity and tree cover change index is to provide additional information from the interaction of climate and land use change by mapping the simultaneous impacts of both of those changes across the conterminous United States. This index illustrates counties with the greatest potential of negative environmental conditions due to concurrent tree cover loss and/or increasing aridity.

To determine areas that have relatively high amounts of environmental and/or climatic changes that are considered to be negative (i.e., tree loss and/or increased aridity), an aridity and tree cover change index was produced. In contrast with the changes in aridity described in the previous section, the changes in aridity from 2000 to 2060 by county were calculated as county aridity value (P/PE) in 2060 minus aridity value in 2000, so that increasing aridity is indicated by negative values, which indicate a negative environmental change. Similarly, changes in percent tree cover were calculated as county percent tree cover in 2060 minus county percent tree cover in 2000 so that the negative environmental change of tree cover loss is indicated by negative values. To calculate the aridity and tree cover change index, tree cover and aridity change values (2000 to 2060 using the decadal averages) were standardized by county across the conterminous United States based on the greatest change observed among all counties (i.e., all county

values were divided by the maximum absolute value of change). In all scenarios, the maximum changes in both percent tree cover (loss of tree cover) and aridity (increasing aridity) were negative numbers, which produced standardized values of change ranging from -1 (greatest negative change) to some positive value less than 1, which indicated increased tree cover and/or decreased aridity. These two standardized values (percent tree cover and aridity) were added and then standardized again to produce values between -1 and some positive value less than 1. With this final standard index value, counties with values approaching -1 indicate areas that have the greatest increase in aridity and/or the greatest decrease in percent tree cover. Counties with positive values indicate areas with decreasing aridity and/or increased percent tree cover.

RESULTS AND DISCUSSION

The following text is divided into sections reporting and discussing the results for tree cover projections, aridity projections, and the combined aridity and tree cover change index for each of the climate change/RPA scenarios.

Projected Tree Cover 2000 to 2060

The percent tree cover for the conterminous United States in 2000 is 34.1 percent, slightly higher than the amount of forest land at 27.1 percent, which reveals the substantial tree cover that exists in the other land uses such as urban and agricultural land. The state with the lowest percent tree cover is North Dakota (3.0 percent), and the state with the greatest percent tree cover is New Hampshire (84.5 percent) (Table 4). The county with the lowest percent tree cover is Greeley County, Kansas (1.0 percent), and the county with the greatest percent tree cover is Hamilton County, New York (94.7 percent) (Fig. 2). As illustrated in Figure 2, the extreme tree-cover values listed above are representative of the regional tree cover in those areas, with many nearby counties and states having very similar values of percent tree cover. That is, these are the expected naturally occurring regional tree cover patterns associated with forest, grassland and desert biomes. For example, the top 10 counties with the highest percent tree cover are in New York, North Carolina, Wisconsin, West Virginia,

Table 4.—Tree cover projections and change for RPA scenarios by state, 2000 to 2060

State	2000 tree cover	2060 RPA scenario A1B tree cover	change[a]	RPA scenario A2 tree cover	change[a]	RPA scenario B2 tree cover	change[a]
	%	%	%	%	%	%	%
Alabama	70.1	67.0	-3.1	67.7	-2.4	68.2	-1.9
Arizona	19.1	19.2	0.1	19.2	0.1	19.2	0.1
Arkansas	55.4	50.6	-4.8	51.8	-3.6	52.1	-3.3
California[b]	35.6	34.2	-1.4	34.2	-1.4	34.6	-1.0
Colorado[c]	24.7	23.1	-1.6	23.2	-1.5	23.6	-1.1
Connecticut	72.0	69.1	-2.9	68.7	-3.3	70.3	-1.7
Delaware	40.8	38.4	-2.4	38.2	-2.6	39.2	-1.6
Florida	54.3	49.7	-4.6	49.3	-5.0	50.6	-3.7
Georgia	66.6	60.0	-6.6	61.6	-5.0	62.1	-4.5
Idaho	39.6	39.2	-0.4	39.3	-0.3	39.4	-0.2
Illinois	16.3	15.8	-0.5	16.0	-0.3	15.9	-0.4
Indiana	27.4	25.1	-2.3	25.8	-1.6	26.0	-1.4
Iowa	11.4	11.2	-0.2	11.3	-0.1	11.2	-0.2
Kansas	7.3	7.3	0.0	7.3	0.0	7.3	0.0
Kentucky	55.4	50.4	-5.0	51.5	-3.9	52.3	-3.1
Louisiana	51.6	48.6	-3.0	49.3	-2.3	49.7	-1.9
Maine	84.4	82.9	-1.5	83.2	-1.2	83.5	-0.9
Maryland[d]	51.3	45.0	-6.3	45.4	-5.9	46.8	-4.5
Massachusetts	69.2	65.1	-4.1	64.7	-4.5	66.5	-2.7
Michigan	59.2	57.3	-1.9	57.6	-1.6	58.0	-1.2
Minnesota	33.7	32.2	-1.5	32.5	-1.2	32.7	-1.0
Mississippi	62.5	59.5	-3.0	60.4	-2.1	60.6	-1.9
Missouri[e]	41.4	38.4	-3.0	39.2	-2.2	39.4	-2.0
Montana	27.3	26.1	-1.2	26.4	-0.9	26.5	-0.8
Nebraska	4.8	4.6	-0.2	4.7	-0.1	4.7	-0.1
Nevada	13.0	12.7	-0.3	12.7	-0.3	12.8	-0.2
New Hampshire	84.5	81.1	-3.4	81.5	-3.0	82.2	-2.3
New Jersey	55.8	48.5	-7.3	47.4	-8.4	50.9	-4.9
New Mexico	18.2	18.0	-0.2	18.0	-0.2	18.0	-0.2
New York	67.0	65.7	-1.3	65.8	-1.2	66.3	-0.7
North Carolina	64.2	60.3	-3.9	60.9	-3.3	61.5	-2.7
North Dakota	3.0	3.0	0.0	3.0	0.0	3.0	0.0
Ohio	39.1	38.2	-0.9	38.3	-0.8	38.6	-0.5
Oklahoma	25.9	24.6	-1.3	24.8	-1.1	25.0	-0.9
Oregon	40.2	39.2	-1.0	39.2	-1.0	39.5	-0.7
Pennsylvania	65.9	63.2	-2.7	63.7	-2.2	64.4	-1.5
Rhode Island	62.5	53.2	-9.3	52.4	-10.1	56.9	-5.6
South Carolina	64.2	60.0	-4.2	60.5	-3.7	61.4	-2.8
South Dakota	4.1	4.3	0.2	4.3	0.2	4.3	0.2
Tennessee	59.3	55.0	-4.3	55.4	-3.9	56.5	-2.8
Texas	21.8	20.6	-1.2	21.1	-0.7	21.0	-0.8
Utah	19.0	17.8	-1.2	17.8	-1.2	18.1	-0.9
Vermont	78.2	74.6	-3.6	75.7	-2.5	75.9	-2.3
Virginia[f]	68.2	65.1	-3.1	65.8	-2.4	66.0	-2.2
Washington	47.3	45.7	-1.6	45.6	-1.7	46.2	-1.1
West Virginia	82.0	77.4	-4.6	79.0	-3.0	79.3	-2.7
Wisconsin	49.0	48.1	-0.9	48.3	-0.7	48.4	-0.6
Wyoming	15.1	14.9	-0.2	14.9	-0.2	15.0	-0.1
Conterminous U.S. total[g]	34.1	32.5	-1.6	32.7	-1.4	33.0	-1.1

[a] Change = (tree cover year 2060 – tree cover year 2000)
[b] California analysis covers 57 of 58 counties of state (Wear 2011)
[c] Colorado analysis covers 62 of 63 counties of state (Wear 2011)
[d] Maryland analysis covers 114 of 115 counties of state (Wear 2011)
[e] Missouri analysis covers 23 of 24 counties of state (Wear 2011)
[f] Virginia analysis covers 97 of 135 counties of state (Wear 2011)
[g] Summary for lower 48 states excluding Washington, D.C.

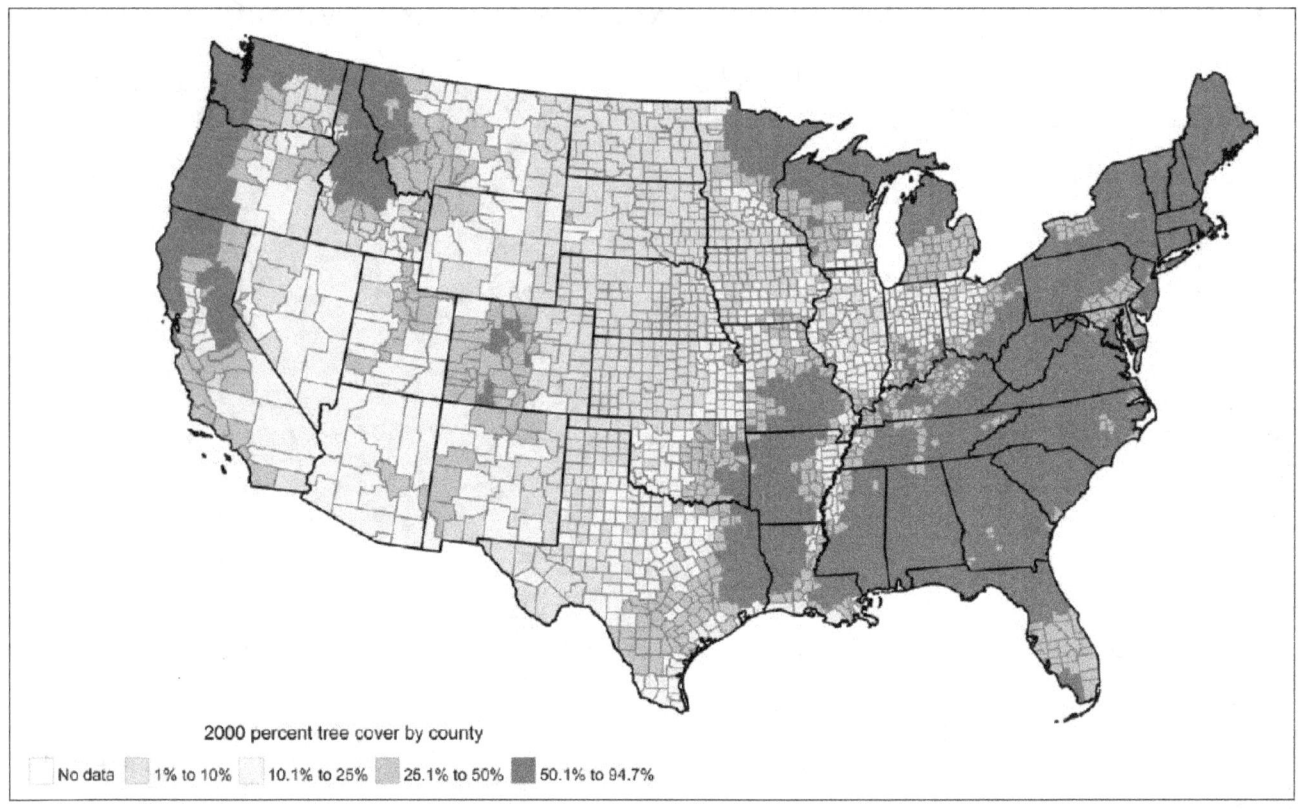

2000 percent tree cover by county

No data	1% to 10%	10.1% to 25%	26.1% to 50%	50.1% to 94.7%

Figure 2.—2000 percent tree cover by county. Maximum and minimum values are represented in the legend.

and New Hampshire, and the next four states behind New Hampshire for the highest percent state tree cover are Maine, West Virginia, Vermont, and Connecticut. The bottom 10 counties with the least percent tree cover are in Kansas, Colorado, Nebraska, and Montana, and the next four states ahead of North Dakota for the lowest percent state tree cover are South Dakota, Nebraska, Kansas, and Iowa (Table 4).

In all three scenarios, percent tree cover in the conterminous United States declines between 2000 and 2060 (Fig. 3). In the RPA A1B scenario, with the largest increase in urbanization, percent tree cover declines by 1.6 percent from 2000 to 32.5 percent (Table 4). The minimum and maximum county percent tree cover also declines from 2000 from a range of 1.0 to 94.7 percent to a range of 0.3 to 93.9 percent. RPA A2 has a decline of 1.4 percent and a range of 0.5 to 94.2 percent tree cover. RPA B2 has a decline of 1.1 percent tree cover with the same range as in RPA A2. These small changes result in little discernible change in the national patterns of tree cover. In all

future scenarios, North Dakota remains the state with the lowest percent tree cover, at 3.0 percent. The bottom five states with the lowest percent tree cover remain the same as 2000 in all three scenarios with very small or no change in 2060. Maine becomes the state with the highest percent tree cover in all three scenarios (82.0 to 83.5 percent) replacing New Hampshire from 2000, but the top five states with the highest percent tree cover remain the same as 2000, each with small decreases in percent tree cover in 2060. In 2060, Phillips County, Colorado, has the lowest percent tree cover in all three scenarios, ranging from 0.3 percent in RPA A1B to 0.5 percent in RPA A2 and B2. Hamilton County, New York, remains the county with the highest percent tree cover in all future scenarios, ranging from 93.9 percent in RPA A1B to 94.2 percent in both RPA A2 and B2. Generally, states that contain the top 10 and bottom 10 counties remain relatively consistent with the 2000 rankings, but with the additions of Michigan, Virginia, and Kentucky for highest percent tree cover, and South Dakota for lowest percent tree cover.

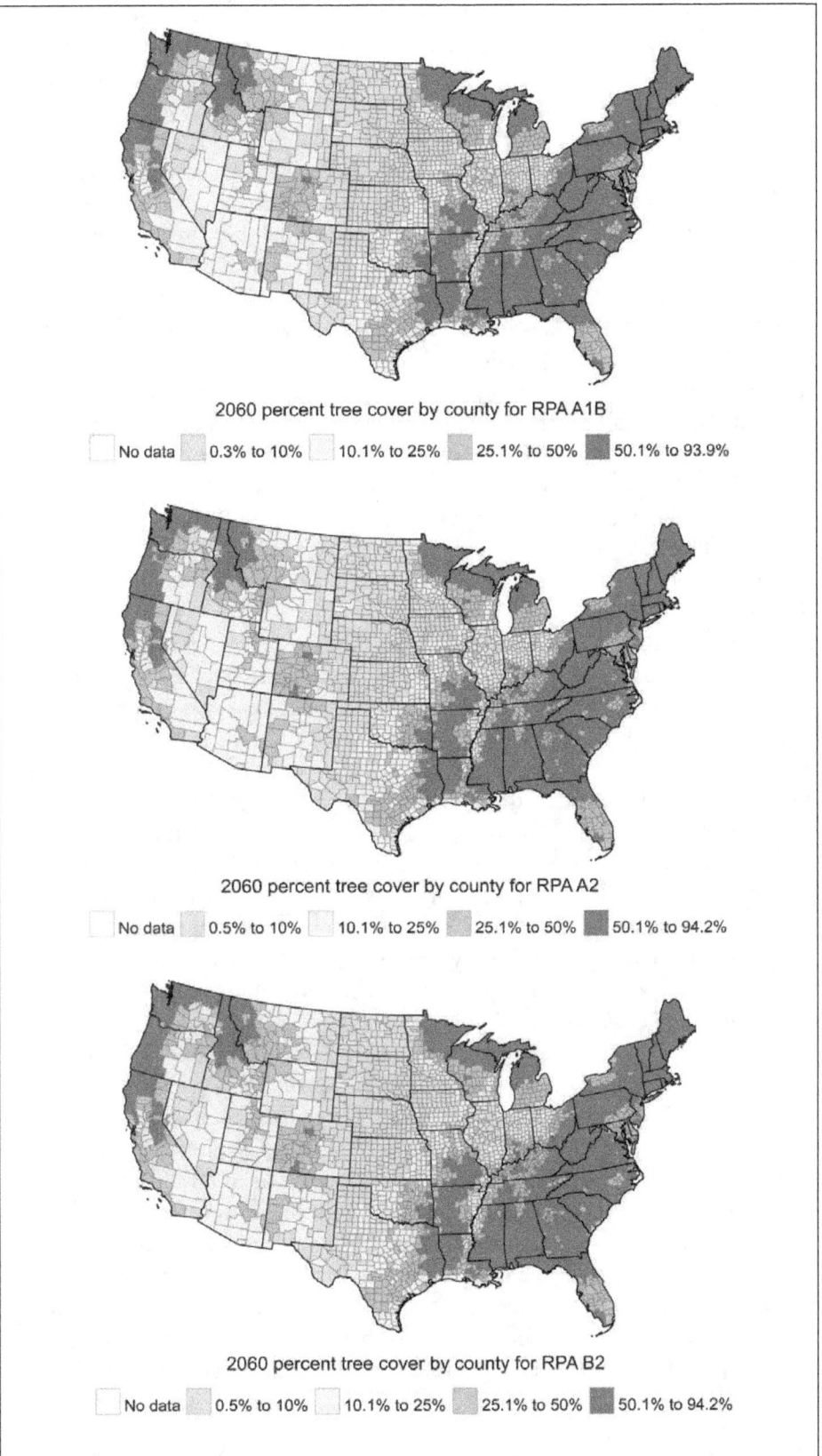

2060 percent tree cover by county for RPA A1B

No data 0.3% to 10% 10.1% to 25% 25.1% to 50% 50.1% to 93.9%

2060 percent tree cover by county for RPA A2

No data 0.5% to 10% 10.1% to 25% 25.1% to 50% 50.1% to 94.2%

2060 percent tree cover by county for RPA B2

No data 0.5% to 10% 10.1% to 25% 25.1% to 50% 50.1% to 94.2%

Figure 3.—2060 percent tree cover by county for RPA scenarios A1B, A2, and B2. Maximum and minimum values are represented in the legends.

The pattern of changes in tree cover is clearer in the figures that display the percent change in tree cover by county (Fig. 4). The greatest loss in percent tree cover for a county across the conterminous United States among all three RPA scenarios is 44.2 percent, and the greatest increase is in the A2 scenario with 15.1 percent. At the state level, South Dakota has the greatest increase in percent tree cover, a small increase of 0.2 percent in all three RPA scenarios (Table 4). Like South Dakota, Arizona has a small increase followed by no changes in Kansas and North Dakota. As illustrated in the figures, most of the increase is minor and found in the grassland and desert regions of the conterminous United States. Rhode Island had the largest decrease in percent tree cover, ranging from 5.6 percent (RPA B2) to 10.1 percent (RPA A2). The highest amount of loss in percent tree cover was found among the heavily forested eastern states of New Jersey, Georgia, Maryland, Florida, and Kentucky. These areas are losing tree cover within and around the urban areas of those states. The county with the greatest loss in percent tree cover between 2000 and 2060 in all three scenarios is Dare County, North Carolina, with a loss of 44.2 percent in all scenarios. The county with the greatest increase in percent tree cover varied by scenario: Lincoln County, Washington, gained 9.2 percent in RPA A1B and 8.1 percent in RPA B2, while Val Verde County, Texas, gained 15.1 percent in RPA A2. Generally, states that contain the top 10 and bottom 10 counties of change include North Carolina, Georgia, Virginia, Maryland, Arkansas, Florida, and New Jersey for the greatest decrease in percent tree cover, and Washington, Texas, Idaho, South Dakota, Wisconsin, and Minnesota for the gains in percent tree cover.

Tree Cover Discussion

Tree cover projections reflect the overall trend of increased urban land use at the expense of forested, agricultural, and other land use categories throughout the conterminous United States in all three RPA scenarios (Wear 2011). In addition, the projections also relate to the original allocation of percent tree cover by land use category in 2000, which is dependent on local and current ecological conditions. In the more forested areas, the percent tree cover tends to decrease with expansion of urban land as tree cover is often displaced with more impervious surfaces or lawn space (e.g., Nowak and Greenfield 2012). In contrast, in grassland and desert areas, urban land use can increase tree cover due to active human management associated with urbanization (e.g., tree planting). However, this projection of increased percent tree cover is often dependent on local ecosystem conditions such as availability of sufficient water resources to sustain tree populations. These tree cover increases may not occur if necessary resources, such as water for irrigation, become scarce. As documented in the RPA Assessment (U.S. Forest Service 2012a), many of the areas projected to increase tree cover, especially in the Intermountain and Great Plains states, are also projected to be vulnerable to water shortage in the future.

Because of the expanding urbanization at the expense of forested and agricultural land uses, the percent tree cover decreases in the more forested counties of the Pacific Northwest and east of the Mississippi River, while the percent tree cover increases in developing grassland and desert counties of the Great Plains and Intermountain regions. In all three RPA scenarios across the conterminous United States, the declines in percent tree cover are of greater frequency and magnitude than the gains in percent tree cover. Generally, the eastern United States loses more forest land than the west because of greater amounts of forest land, higher population density, higher urbanization, and lower amounts of protected forest lands. The exceptions are the areas of higher population densities in the west, and areas that project low density development into rural areas neighboring protected forest lands. The implications of this development include concerns for declining forest inventories and carbon stocks, habitat loss and degradation, and increased competition for goods and services from the natural ecosystems. In addition, areas of urban forest will increase and have greater competition for their ecosystem services (U.S. Forest Service 2012a).

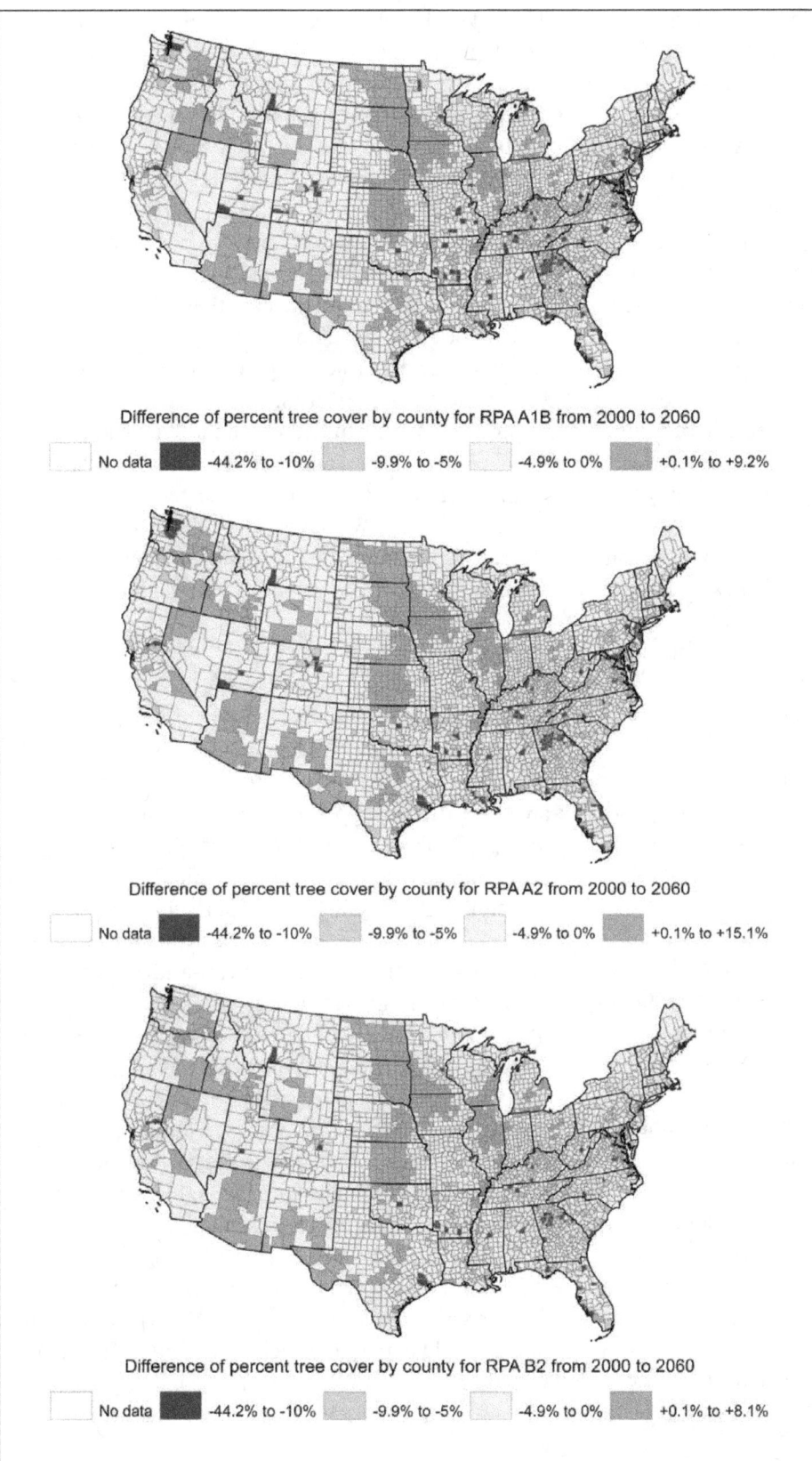

Difference of percent tree cover by county for RPA A1B from 2000 to 2060

No data | -44.2% to -10% | -9.9% to -5% | -4.9% to 0% | +0.1% to +9.2%

Difference of percent tree cover by county for RPA A2 from 2000 to 2060

No data | -44.2% to -10% | -9.9% to -5% | -4.9% to 0% | +0.1% to +15.1%

Difference of percent tree cover by county for RPA B2 from 2000 to 2060

No data | -44.2% to -10% | -9.9% to -5% | -4.9% to 0% | +0.1% to +8.1%

Figure 4.—Difference of percent tree cover by county for RPA scenarios A1B, A2, and B2 from 2000 to 2060. Maximum and minimum values are represented in the legends.

The largest decline in forest land is in the South Region (up to 21 million acres) (U.S. Forest Service 2012a), and this analysis reflects those higher magnitude tree cover losses (maximum tree cover loss of 44.2 percent among all three RPA scenarios) in and around the established and growing urban regions found within heavily tree covered and rapidly urbanizing regions such as metropolitan Atlanta, Georgia, which has several counties projected to lose 20 percent or more of their tree cover in all three RPA scenarios.

In contrast, the expansion of development in the desert and grassland regions may increase tree cover, but the magnitude of increases is less (maximum tree cover gain ranges from 15.1 to 8.1 percent at the county scale among the three RPA scenarios) than the losses illustrated above. For example, three developing rural counties in the eastern region of South Dakota have a range of increases across the three scenarios of 2.5 to 4.3 percent. However, these increases may not be realized due to projected increases in competition for water resources.

The tree cover projections assume that the average percent tree cover within a county land cover class will remain constant through time, as well as the current natural resource policies and ecosystem conditions. Though the use of average cover by land use type can provide reasonable projections, there are various conditions or factors that may change to alter these projections. These factors include changes in aridity/climate in the future that may affect regeneration and the ability or desire to water urban trees, future storms, wildfires, or insect outbreaks that can lead to significant losses in tree cover, and tree planting campaigns or natural resource protection policies that may stabilize and/or increase tree cover. The greater the deviation from current and recent past conditions, and from the projected land cover changes, the more the projected cover estimates will vary from the given projections.

All three scenarios exhibit similar patterns of future changes in percent tree cover across the United States.

The RPA A1B scenario, which has the most urban development outside of the more urbanized counties, has the largest change with a 1.6 percent decrease in tree cover in the conterminous United States from 2000 to 2060. The B2 scenario, which has the most urban growth within the already urbanized counties, has the smallest change, with a 1.1 percent decrease. Even though tree cover changes within a state or nationwide are relatively small (mostly less than 10 percent), changes at the county level can be much higher and more variable. For example, the county with the greatest projected percent tree cover loss, Dare County, North Carolina, loses tree cover because of projected urban and other land use increases at the expense of forest and agricultural land uses. The counties projected to gain the most percent tree cover (Lincoln County, WA, and Val Verde County, TX) had increased cover mostly due to projected increases in urban land in Lincoln County and agricultural land in Val Verde County.

Projected Aridity 2000 to 2060

In 2000, the aridity ratio (P/PE) for the conterminous United States is 0.49, or semi-arid (Table 5). In 2000, the conterminous United States has 0.5 percent of its area classified as hyperarid, 26.3 percent as arid, 35.3 percent as semi-arid, 25.2 percent as dry subhumid, and 12.8 percent as humid (Table 6). Generally, the hyperarid and arid regions are found in the Intermountain region and extending from west Texas to southern California. Semi-arid areas are found in the Southeast, a large percentage of the center of the conterminous United States, and scattered in a crescent pattern from the Intermountain region into Pacific Coast states. Dry subhumid regions cover the eastern states, and humid areas are found along the northern Pacific coast, western Rocky Mountains, northern Gulf coast, and into the highlands of the eastern states. The most arid state is Arizona at 0.10 (arid), and the least arid state is Washington at 0.97 (humid). Imperial County, California, is the most arid county, with an aridity value of 0.02 (hyperarid), while the least arid county is Jefferson County, Washington, with a value of 3.15 (humid) (Fig. 5).

Table 5.—Aridity projections and change for RPA scenario-climate combinations by state, 2000 to 2060

State	2000[a] aridity[c]	CGCM3.1 aridity[c]	CGCM3.1 change[d]	CSIRO-Mk3.5 aridity[c]	CSIRO-Mk3.5 change[d]	MIROC3.2 aridity[c]	MIROC3.2 change[d]
Alabama	0.61	0.54	0.07	0.54	0.07	0.34	0.27
Arizona	0.10	0.09	0.01	0.10	0.00	0.07	0.03
Arkansas	0.54	0.50	0.04	0.44	0.10	0.29	0.25
California	0.40	0.32	0.08	0.34	0.06	0.32	0.08
Colorado	0.24	0.22	0.02	0.21	0.03	0.15	0.09
Connecticut	0.78	0.68	0.10	0.64	0.14	0.64	0.14
Delaware	0.63	0.55	0.08	0.55	0.08	0.45	0.18
District of Columbia	0.57	0.51	0.06	0.53	0.04	0.40	0.17
Florida	0.54	0.50	0.04	0.56	-0.02	0.25	0.29
Georgia	0.53	0.50	0.03	0.51	0.02	0.30	0.23
Idaho	0.35	0.33	0.02	0.32	0.03	0.28	0.07
Illinois	0.53	0.46	0.07	0.39	0.14	0.31	0.22
Indiana	0.60	0.49	0.11	0.45	0.15	0.35	0.25
Iowa	0.46	0.44	0.02	0.37	0.09	0.29	0.17
Kansas	0.32	0.29	0.03	0.25	0.07	0.19	0.13
Kentucky	0.63	0.53	0.10	0.52	0.11	0.38	0.25
Louisiana	0.61	0.55	0.06	0.55	0.06	0.33	0.28
Maine	0.78	0.70	0.08	0.71	0.07	0.66	0.12
Maryland	0.62	0.54	0.08	0.55	0.07	0.43	0.19
Massachusetts	0.78	0.68	0.10	0.64	0.14	0.64	0.14
Michigan	0.57	0.48	0.09	0.45	0.12	0.35	0.22
Minnesota	0.43	0.41	0.02	0.35	0.08	0.30	0.13
Mississippi	0.62	0.54	0.08	0.53	0.09	0.34	0.28
Missouri	0.51	0.45	0.06	0.37	0.14	0.28	0.23
Montana	0.27	0.28	-0.01	0.25	0.02	0.23	0.04
Nebraska	0.29	0.30	-0.01	0.27	0.02	0.19	0.10
Nevada	0.13	0.12	0.01	0.13	0.00	0.10	0.03
New Hampshire	0.77	0.67	0.10	0.64	0.13	0.63	0.14
New Jersey	0.67	0.61	0.06	0.60	0.07	0.53	0.14
New Mexico	0.14	0.12	0.02	0.13	0.01	0.09	0.05
New York	0.71	0.61	0.10	0.58	0.13	0.52	0.19
North Carolina	0.61	0.56	0.05	0.57	0.04	0.40	0.21
North Dakota	0.28	0.27	0.01	0.20	0.08	0.20	0.08
Ohio	0.60	0.49	0.11	0.46	0.14	0.37	0.23
Oklahoma	0.37	0.32	0.05	0.30	0.07	0.21	0.16
Oregon	0.86	0.78	0.08	0.71	0.15	0.73	0.13
Pennsylvania	0.69	0.60	0.09	0.59	0.10	0.48	0.21
Rhode Island	0.79	0.70	0.09	0.66	0.13	0.66	0.13
South Carolina	0.51	0.50	0.01	0.53	-0.02	0.32	0.19
South Dakota	0.29	0.29	0.00	0.23	0.06	0.19	0.10
Tennessee	0.67	0.57	0.10	0.58	0.09	0.38	0.29
Texas	0.30	0.27	0.03	0.25	0.05	0.16	0.14
Utah	0.21	0.20	0.01	0.19	0.02	0.14	0.07
Vermont	0.77	0.66	0.11	0.65	0.12	0.61	0.16
Virginia	0.59	0.52	0.07	0.52	0.07	0.39	0.20
Washington	0.97	0.87	0.10	0.76	0.21	0.81	0.16
West Virginia	0.66	0.56	0.10	0.56	0.10	0.42	0.24
Wisconsin	0.53	0.46	0.07	0.44	0.09	0.34	0.19
Wyoming	0.23	0.23	0.00	0.20	0.03	0.15	0.08
Conterminous U.S.[e]	0.49	0.44	0.05	0.41	0.08	0.30	0.19

[a] 2000 is the modeled base year (annual values from decadal average of 1995 to 2004)

[b] 2060 is the modeled year for projections (annual values from decadal average of 2055 to 2064)

[c] Aridity is the ratio of precipitation (P) to potential evapotranspiration (PET); P/PE (Middleton and Thomas, 1997)

[d] Change = aridity 2000 – aridity 2060

[e] Summary for lower 48 states including Washington, DC

(Table 5 continued on next page)

Table 5 (continued).

| State | 2000[a] aridity[c] | 2060[b] A2 | | | | | |
| | | CGCM3.1 | | CSIRO-Mk3.5 | | MIROC3.2 | |
		aridity[c]	change[d]	aridity[c]	change[d]	aridity[c]	change[d]
Alabama	0.61	0.47	0.14	0.57	0.04	0.39	0.22
Arizona	0.10	0.09	0.01	0.12	-0.02	0.07	0.03
Arkansas	0.54	0.44	0.10	0.52	0.02	0.30	0.24
California	0.40	0.26	0.14	0.39	0.01	0.30	0.10
Colorado	0.24	0.20	0.04	0.23	0.01	0.17	0.07
Connecticut	0.78	0.68	0.10	0.60	0.18	0.67	0.11
Delaware	0.63	0.54	0.09	0.47	0.16	0.47	0.16
District of Columbia	0.57	0.50	0.07	0.44	0.13	0.42	0.15
Florida	0.54	0.44	0.10	0.48	0.06	0.29	0.25
Georgia	0.53	0.43	0.10	0.50	0.03	0.35	0.18
Idaho	0.35	0.31	0.04	0.33	0.02	0.28	0.07
Illinois	0.53	0.43	0.10	0.52	0.01	0.34	0.19
Indiana	0.60	0.48	0.12	0.56	0.04	0.39	0.21
Iowa	0.46	0.39	0.07	0.44	0.02	0.31	0.15
Kansas	0.32	0.26	0.06	0.30	0.02	0.20	0.12
Kentucky	0.63	0.52	0.11	0.56	0.07	0.40	0.23
Louisiana	0.61	0.49	0.12	0.53	0.08	0.36	0.25
Maine	0.78	0.69	0.09	0.67	0.11	0.71	0.07
Maryland	0.62	0.53	0.09	0.47	0.15	0.45	0.17
Massachusetts	0.78	0.68	0.10	0.60	0.18	0.68	0.10
Michigan	0.57	0.45	0.12	0.49	0.08	0.43	0.14
Minnesota	0.43	0.36	0.07	0.38	0.05	0.31	0.12
Mississippi	0.62	0.47	0.15	0.56	0.06	0.37	0.25
Missouri	0.51	0.41	0.10	0.47	0.04	0.30	0.21
Montana	0.27	0.27	0.00	0.28	-0.01	0.23	0.04
Nebraska	0.29	0.28	0.01	0.30	-0.01	0.20	0.09
Nevada	0.13	0.09	0.04	0.15	-0.02	0.09	0.04
New Hampshire	0.77	0.66	0.11	0.61	0.16	0.68	0.09
New Jersey	0.67	0.61	0.06	0.53	0.14	0.55	0.12
New Mexico	0.14	0.12	0.02	0.16	-0.02	0.09	0.05
New York	0.71	0.59	0.12	0.57	0.14	0.56	0.15
North Carolina	0.61	0.52	0.09	0.53	0.08	0.42	0.19
North Dakota	0.28	0.26	0.02	0.25	0.03	0.22	0.06
Ohio	0.60	0.49	0.11	0.54	0.06	0.41	0.19
Oklahoma	0.37	0.29	0.08	0.33	0.04	0.20	0.17
Oregon	0.86	0.73	0.13	0.71	0.15	0.74	0.12
Pennsylvania	0.69	0.59	0.10	0.58	0.11	0.52	0.17
Rhode Island	0.79	0.70	0.09	0.61	0.18	0.70	0.09
South Carolina	0.51	0.45	0.06	0.48	0.03	0.35	0.16
South Dakota	0.29	0.27	0.02	0.25	0.04	0.20	0.09
Tennessee	0.67	0.53	0.14	0.60	0.07	0.41	0.26
Texas	0.30	0.24	0.06	0.29	0.01	0.15	0.15
Utah	0.21	0.16	0.05	0.22	-0.01	0.15	0.06
Vermont	0.77	0.64	0.13	0.62	0.15	0.66	0.11
Virginia	0.59	0.50	0.09	0.46	0.13	0.41	0.18
Washington	0.97	0.85	0.12	0.77	0.20	0.79	0.18
West Virginia	0.66	0.55	0.11	0.55	0.11	0.45	0.21
Wisconsin	0.53	0.41	0.12	0.47	0.06	0.38	0.15
Wyoming	0.23	0.21	0.02	0.22	0.01	0.17	0.06
Conterminous U.S.[e]	0.49	0.40	0.09	0.44	0.05	0.32	0.17

[a] 2000 is the modeled base year (annual values from decadal average of 1995 to 2004)

[b] 2060 is the modeled year for projections (annual values from decadal average of 2055 to 2064)

[c] Aridity is the ratio of precipitation (P) to potential evapotranspiration (PET); P/PE (Middleton and Thomas, 1997)

[d] Change = aridity 2000 − aridity 2060

[e] Summary for lower 48 states including Washington, DC

(Table 5 continued on next page)

Table 5 (continued).

State	2000[a] aridity[c]	2060[b] B2 CGCM2 aridity[c]	2060[b] B2 CGCM2 change[d]	2060[b] B2 CSIRO-Mk2 aridity[c]	2060[b] B2 CSIRO-Mk2 change[d]	2060[b] B2 HADCM3 aridity[c]	2060[b] B2 HADCM3 change[d]
Alabama	0.61	0.47	0.14	0.52	0.09	0.54	0.07
Arizona	0.10	0.09	0.01	0.08	0.02	0.12	-0.02
Arkansas	0.54	0.44	0.10	0.40	0.14	0.42	0.12
California	0.40	0.35	0.05	0.28	0.12	0.27	0.13
Colorado	0.24	0.20	0.04	0.19	0.05	0.22	0.02
Connecticut	0.78	0.65	0.13	0.65	0.13	0.67	0.11
Delaware	0.63	0.48	0.15	0.52	0.11	0.54	0.09
District of Columbia	0.57	0.43	0.14	0.48	0.09	0.50	0.07
Florida	0.54	0.44	0.10	0.47	0.07	0.50	0.04
Georgia	0.53	0.42	0.11	0.48	0.05	0.51	0.02
Idaho	0.35	0.31	0.04	0.32	0.03	0.28	0.07
Illinois	0.53	0.38	0.15	0.43	0.10	0.43	0.10
Indiana	0.60	0.42	0.18	0.48	0.12	0.48	0.12
Iowa	0.46	0.37	0.09	0.35	0.11	0.35	0.11
Kansas	0.32	0.23	0.09	0.22	0.10	0.25	0.07
Kentucky	0.63	0.42	0.21	0.52	0.11	0.54	0.09
Louisiana	0.61	0.56	0.05	0.50	0.11	0.49	0.12
Maine	0.78	0.71	0.07	0.67	0.11	0.68	0.10
Maryland	0.62	0.46	0.16	0.51	0.11	0.53	0.09
Massachusetts	0.78	0.66	0.12	0.65	0.13	0.68	0.10
Michigan	0.57	0.46	0.11	0.43	0.14	0.45	0.12
Minnesota	0.43	0.36	0.07	0.29	0.14	0.32	0.11
Mississippi	0.62	0.50	0.12	0.50	0.12	0.51	0.11
Missouri	0.51	0.35	0.16	0.37	0.14	0.39	0.12
Montana	0.27	0.24	0.03	0.24	0.03	0.23	0.04
Nebraska	0.29	0.23	0.06	0.23	0.06	0.22	0.07
Nevada	0.13	0.12	0.01	0.11	0.02	0.12	0.01
New Hampshire	0.77	0.66	0.11	0.64	0.13	0.65	0.12
New Jersey	0.67	0.55	0.12	0.58	0.09	0.60	0.07
New Mexico	0.14	0.11	0.03	0.11	0.03	0.14	0.00
New York	0.71	0.57	0.14	0.58	0.13	0.58	0.13
North Carolina	0.61	0.47	0.14	0.54	0.07	0.58	0.03
North Dakota	0.28	0.23	0.05	0.19	0.09	0.20	0.08
Ohio	0.60	0.41	0.19	0.48	0.12	0.49	0.11
Oklahoma	0.37	0.29	0.08	0.24	0.13	0.28	0.09
Oregon	0.86	0.77	0.09	0.64	0.22	0.54	0.32
Pennsylvania	0.69	0.52	0.17	0.57	0.12	0.58	0.11
Rhode Island	0.79	0.67	0.12	0.66	0.13	0.70	0.09
South Carolina	0.51	0.41	0.10	0.48	0.03	0.51	0.00
South Dakota	0.29	0.23	0.06	0.20	0.09	0.20	0.09
Tennessee	0.67	0.46	0.21	0.54	0.13	0.57	0.10
Texas	0.30	0.26	0.04	0.22	0.08	0.23	0.07
Utah	0.21	0.18	0.03	0.19	0.02	0.21	0.00
Vermont	0.77	0.66	0.11	0.65	0.12	0.63	0.14
Virginia	0.59	0.42	0.17	0.49	0.10	0.52	0.07
Washington	0.97	0.85	0.12	0.70	0.27	0.58	0.39
West Virginia	0.66	0.44	0.22	0.53	0.13	0.57	0.09
Wisconsin	0.53	0.44	0.09	0.39	0.14	0.40	0.13
Wyoming	0.23	0.21	0.02	0.20	0.03	0.20	0.03
Conterminous U.S.[e]	0.49	0.38	0.11	0.39	0.10	0.40	0.09

[a] 2000 is the modeled base year (annual values from decadal average of 1995 to 2004)
[b] 2060 is the modeled year for projections (annual values from decadal average of 2055 to 2064)
[c] Aridity is the ratio of precipitation (P) to potential evapotranspiration (PET); P/PE (Middleton and Thomas, 1997)
[d] Change = aridity 2000 – aridity 2060
[e] Summary for lower 48 states including Washington, DC

Table 6.—Land area distribution of categories of aridity for the conterminous United States, 2000 to 2060

| Aridity Class | 2000 percent[a] | 2060 A1B | | | | | |
| | | CGCM3.1 | | CSIRO-Mk3.5 | | MIROC3.2 | |
		percent[a]	change[b]	percent[a]	change[b]	percent[a]	change[b]
Hyperarid	0.5	1.7	1.2	1.4	0.9	2.5	2.0
Arid	26.3	26.8	0.5	32.1	5.8	39.0	12.7
Semi-arid	35.3	45.8	10.5	41.5	6.2	49.7	14.4
Dry subhumid	25.2	19.1	-6.1	19.5	-5.7	5.1	-20.1
Humid	12.8	6.6	-6.2	5.6	-7.2	3.7	-9.1

[a] Values calculated for conterminous U.S. including Washington, D.C. from counties within each aridity ratio category
[b] Change = year 2060 values − year 2000 values

| Aridity Class | 2000 percent[a] | 2060 A2 | | | | | |
| | | CGCM3.1 | | CSIRO-Mk3.5 | | MIROC3.2 | |
		percent[a]	change[b]	percent[a]	change[b]	percent[a]	change[b]
Hyperarid	0.5	2.4	1.9	0.5	0.0	2.5	2.0
Arid	26.3	30.0	3.7	25.6	-0.7	38.0	11.7
Semi-arid	35.3	50.3	15.0	46.6	11.3	49.8	14.5
Dry subhumid	25.2	11.9	-13.3	21.6	-3.6	5.0	-20.2
Humid	12.8	5.4	-7.4	5.7	-7.1	4.6	-8.2

[a] Values calculated for conterminous U.S. including Washington, D.C. from counties within each aridity ratio category
[b] Change = year 2060 values − year 2000 values

| Aridity Class | 2000 percent[a] | 2060 B2 | | | | | |
| | | CGCM2 | | CSIRO-Mk2 | | HADCM3 | |
		percent[a]	change[b]	percent[a]	change[b]	percent[a]	change[b]
Hyperarid	0.5	1.4	0.9	1.7	1.2	0.3	-0.2
Arid	26.3	31.5	5.2	35.4	9.1	35.5	9.2
Semi-arid	35.3	53.0	17.7	45.0	9.7	42.9	7.6
Dry subhumid	25.2	9.1	-16.1	13.3	-11.9	16.9	-8.3
Humid	12.8	4.9	-7.9	4.6	-8.2	4.3	-8.5

[a] Values calculated for conterminous U.S. including Washington, D.C. from counties within each aridity ratio category
[b] Change = year 2060 values − year 2000 values

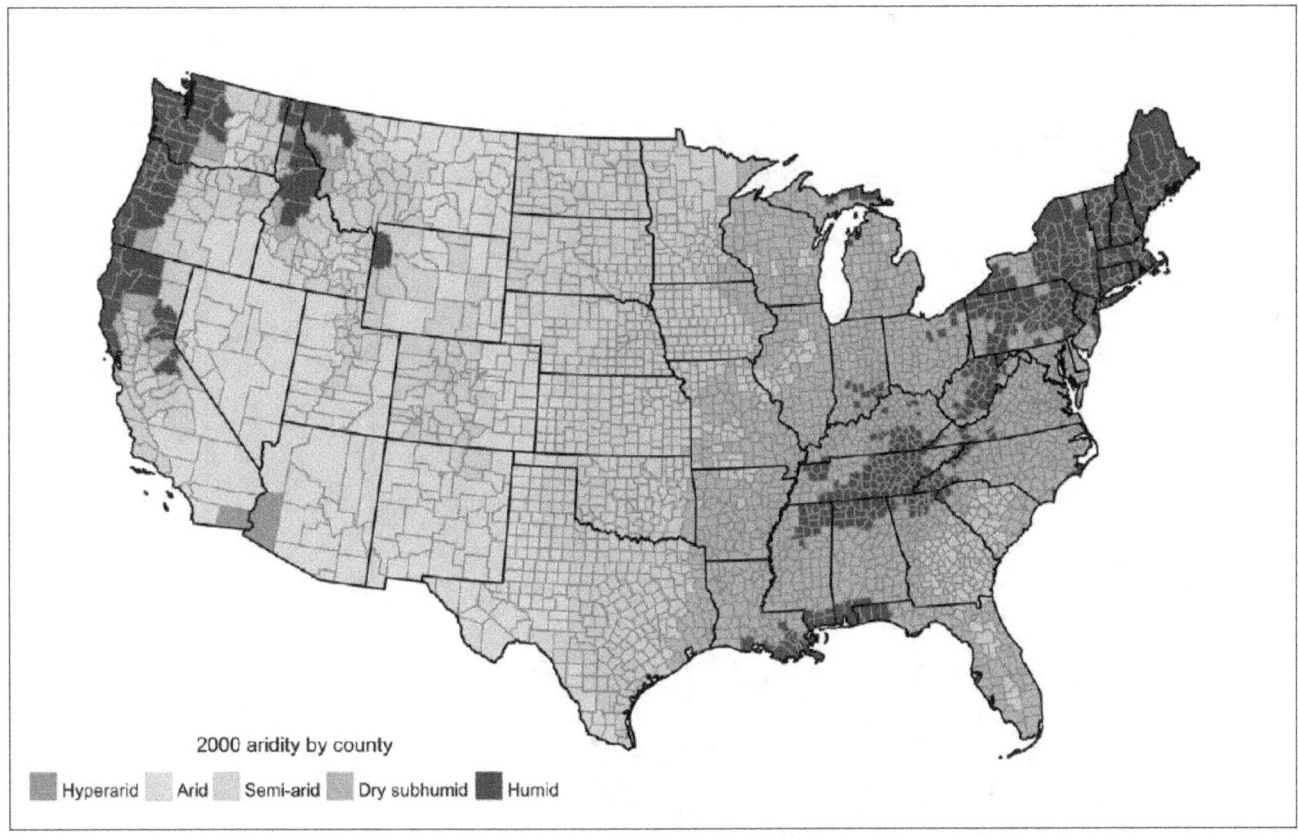

Figure 5.—2000 aridity by county

Scenario RPA A1B

Across all three climate projection models in RPA A1B, aridity of the conterminous United States is projected to increase between 2000 and 2060. The projected aridity (P/PE) ranges from 0.30 (an increase of 0.19) from the MIROC3.2 model to 0.44 (an increase of 0.05) from the CGCM3.1 model (Table 5). Despite the change in aridity ratio for the conterminous United States, the aridity class remains the same: semi-arid. Regionally, the changes indicated by aridity class conversion occur in the pattern described below with less conversion in CGCM3.1 to the most conversion in MIROC3.2 projections (Fig. 6). Generally, aridity classes convert to more arid classes in a west to east pattern, with hyperarid conversions from arid in the southwest, arid conversions from semi-arid in the Great Plains and Intermountain states, semi-arid conversion from dry subhumid in the North Central to the South Central states, and dry subhumid conversion from humid in the East.

In 2060, the area of hyperarid land of the conterminous United States is projected to increase in all three models ranging from a 2.0 percent increase in the MIROC3.2 results to a 0.9 percent increase in the CSIRO-Mk3.5 model (Table 6). Arid land increases in all three projections, ranging from a 12.7 percent rise in the MIROC3.2 results to a 0.5 percent increase in the CGCM3.1 projection. Semi-arid land grows in all three models, ranging from a 14.4 percent increase with the MIROC3.2 projection to 6.2 percent growth in the CSIRO-Mk3.5 results. Dry subhumid land area decreases among all models, ranging from a 20.1 percent reduction in the MIROC3.2 results to a 5.7 percent reduction in the CSIRO-Mk3.5 projection. Humid land area also decreases in the three projections, ranging from a 9.1 percent decline in the MIROC3.2 results to a 6.2 percent decrease in the CGCM3.1 model.

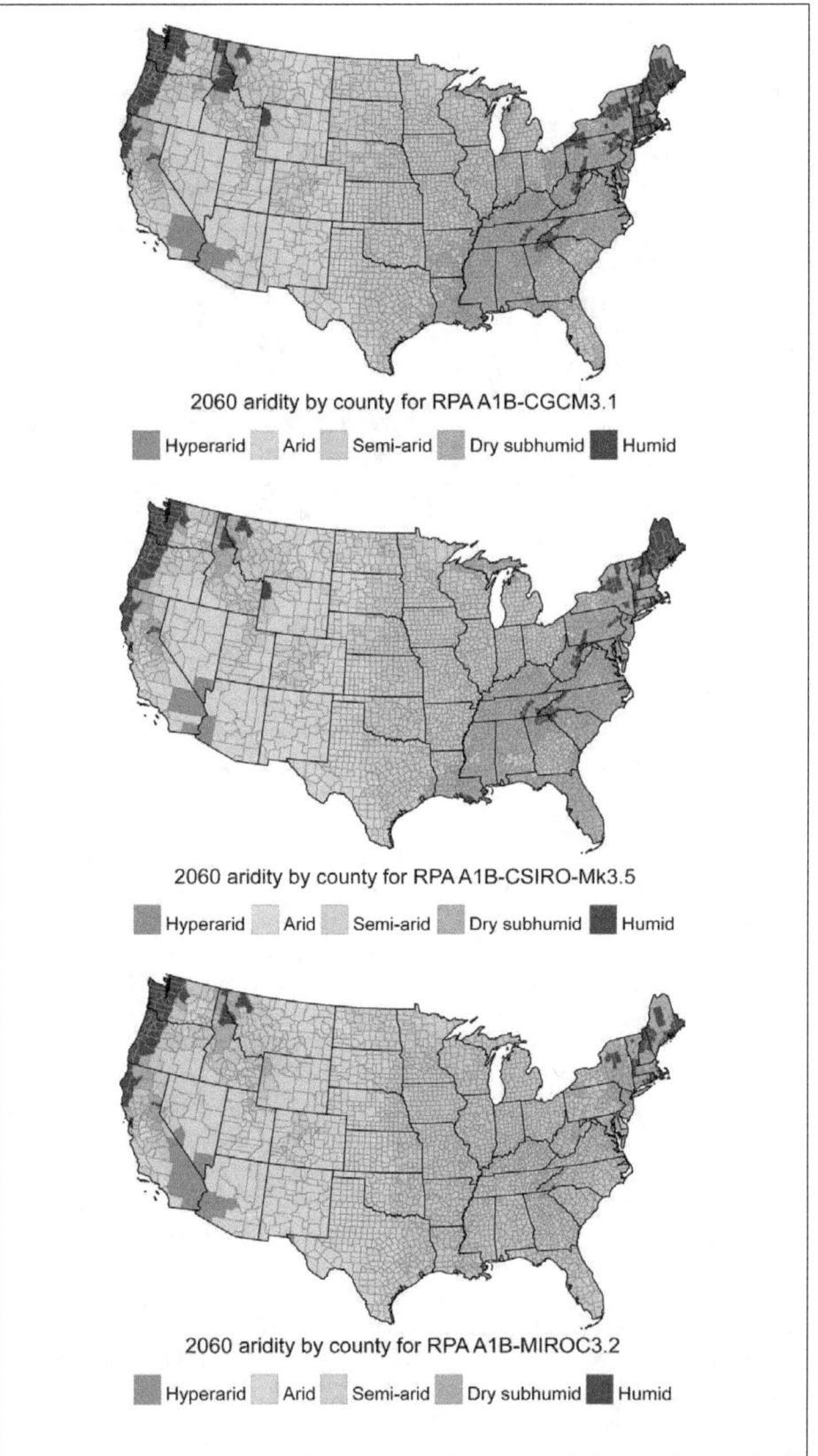

2060 aridity by county for RPA A1B-CGCM3.1

Hyperarid　Arid　Semi-arid　Dry subhumid　Humid

2060 aridity by county for RPA A1B-CSIRO-Mk3.5

Hyperarid　Arid　Semi-arid　Dry subhumid　Humid

2060 aridity by county for RPA A1B-MIROC3.2

Hyperarid　Arid　Semi-arid　Dry subhumid　Humid

Figure 6.—2060 aridity by county for RPA A1B-CGCM3.1, A1B-CSIRO-Mk3.5, and A1B-MIROC3.2

Arizona is projected to remain the most arid state in all three models with no change from 2000 in the CSIRO-Mk3.5 results to a 0.03 increase in aridity in the MIROC3.2 projection, but with no change in aridity class (Table 5). Washington is projected to continue as the least arid state with no change in aridity class, but all models project increasing aridity in that state ranging from a 0.21 change in the CSIRO-Mk3.5 model to a 0.10 change in the CGCM3.1 results.

Imperial County, California, continues to be the most arid county projected in all three 2060 projections with an aridity ratio of 0.02 (no change from 2000) (Fig. 6). The least arid county among all three models in 2060 continues to be Jefferson County, Washington, but its aridity is increasing from 2000, ranging from a change of 0.62 in the CSIRO-Mk3.5 results to a 0.26 difference in the CGCM3.1 projection. With these changes the county does not change its aridity class.

Increases of aridity from 2000 to 2060 are of greater magnitude and frequency than decreases of aridity and were variable across the United States (Fig. 7). In model CGCM3.1, aridity changes between -0.04 to 0.48, and the greatest change (increase of aridity) is found in Pacific Northwest. The results from CSIRO-Mk3.5 have the greatest range of the three models; -0.08 to 0.66 with the greatest change (increase of aridity) also found in the Pacific Northwest. The MIROC3.2 projection has a range of 0.00 to 0.58 with no counties of decreasing aridity. In addition to the greatest aridity increases projected in the Pacific Northwest, the model projects a substantial increase of aridity extending from the Gulf of Mexico coast to the north through the South and North Central states.

The counties with the greatest increase of aridity are Tillamook County, Oregon, in the CGCM3.1 projection and Skamania County, Washington, in both CSIRO-Mk3.5 and MIROC3.2 models, with increases of 0.66 and 0.58, respectively. In both cases, aridity class does not change. In the CGCM3.1 model, the county with the greatest decrease in aridity is Nance County, Nebraska, with a change of -0.04 (no change in aridity class). In the CSIRO-Mk3.5 projection, the greatest decrease in aridity is Volusia County,

Florida, a change of -0.08 (no change in aridity class). In the MIROC3.2 model, there are no counties with decreases in aridity.

Scenario RPA A2

Aridity in the conterminous United States is projected to increase between 2000 and 2060 across all three climate projections in RPA A2. The projected aridity ratio (P/PE) in 2060 ranges from 0.32 (an increase of 0.17) from the MIROC3.2 model to 0.44 (an increase of 0.05) from the CSIRO-Mk3.5 results (Table 5). The aridity class of the conterminous United States remains the same: semi-arid. The pattern of aridity class change is similar to RPA scenario A1B (Fig. 8). The least amount of change occurs in the CSIRO-Mk3.5 model and the most in the MIROC 3.2 model.

In 2060, the area of hyperarid land of the conterminous United States is projected to increase in two models ranging from a 2.0 percent increase in the MIROC3.2 forecast to a 1.9 percent increase in the CGCM3.1 model (Table 6). In the CSIRO-Mk3.5 results, there is no change from 2000. Arid land increases in two projections, ranging from an 11.7 percent rise in the MIROC3.2 results to a 3.7 percent increase in the CGCM3.1 model. In the CSIRO-Mk3.5 projection, arid land decreases 0.7 percent. Semi-arid land area increases in all three models, ranging from a 15.0 percent increase with the CGCM3.1 projection to 11.3 percent growth in the CSIRO-Mk3.5 results. Dry subhumid land area decreases in all models, ranging from a 20.2 percent reduction in the MIROC3.2 model to a 3.6 percent reduction in the CSIRO-Mk3.5 projection. Humid land area also decreases in the three projections, ranging from an 8.2 percent decline in the MIROC3.2 results to a 7.1 percent decrease in the CSIRO-Mk3.5 model.

In two projections, Arizona continues to be the most arid state, and in the CGCM3.1 model it is tied with Nevada as the most arid (Table 5). In the CSIRO-Mk3.5 results, Arizona is projected to become slightly less arid, a 0.02 decrease, but in the other two models the state becomes more arid, with a 0.01 increase in the CGCM3.1 projection results and a 0.03 increase in the MIROC3.2 model. Nevada's change is projected

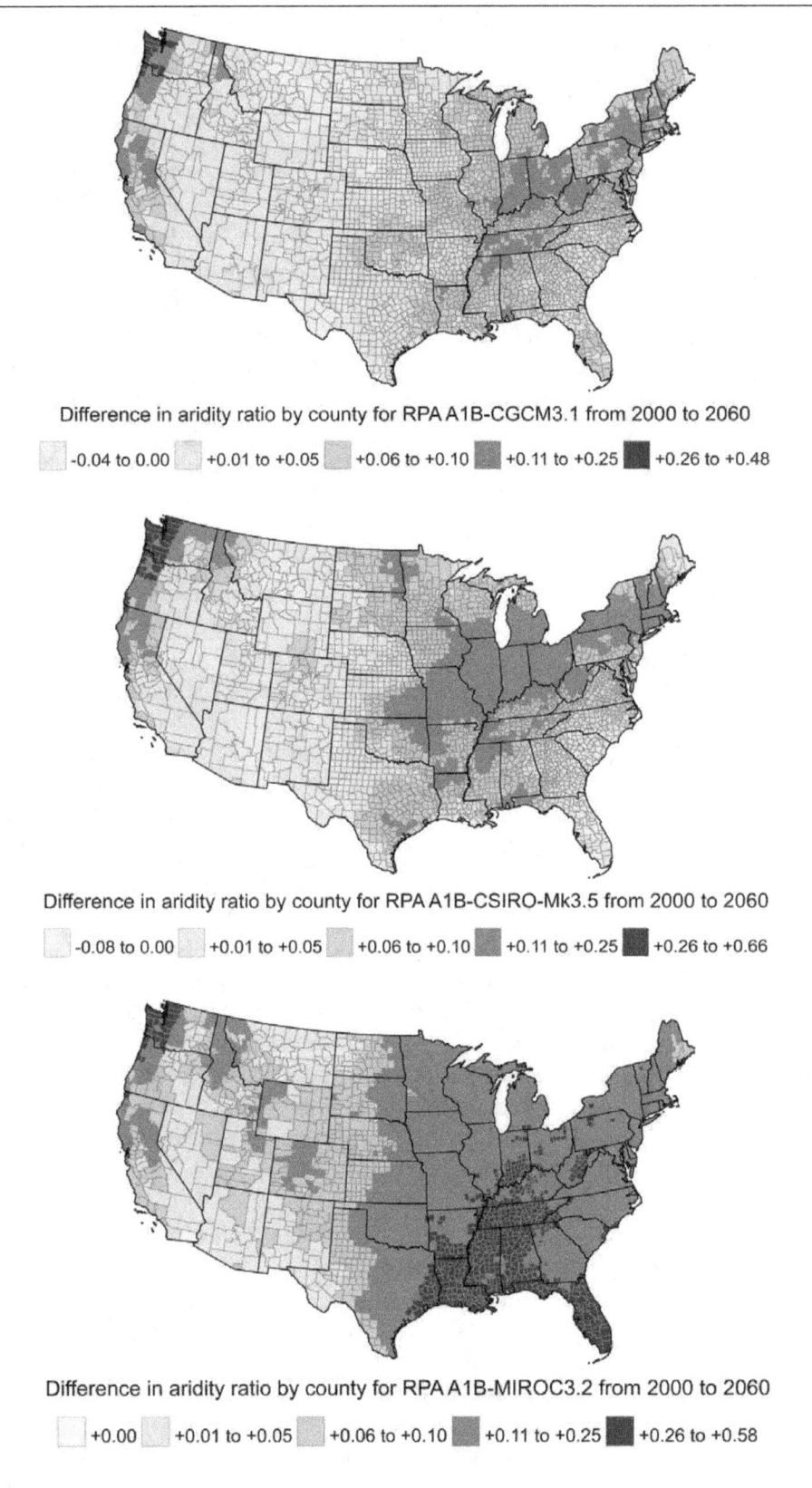

Difference in aridity ratio by county for RPA A1B-CGCM3.1 from 2000 to 2060

-0.04 to 0.00   +0.01 to +0.05   +0.06 to +0.10   +0.11 to +0.25   +0.26 to +0.48

Difference in aridity ratio by county for RPA A1B-CSIRO-Mk3.5 from 2000 to 2060

-0.08 to 0.00   +0.01 to +0.05   +0.06 to +0.10   +0.11 to +0.25   +0.26 to +0.66

Difference in aridity ratio by county for RPA A1B-MIROC3.2 from 2000 to 2060

+0.00   +0.01 to +0.05   +0.06 to +0.10   +0.11 to +0.25   +0.26 to +0.58

Figure 7.—Difference in aridity ratio by county for RPA A1B-CGCM3.1, A1B-CSIRO-Mk3.5, and A1B-MIROC3.2 from 2000 to 2060. Maximum and minimum values are represented in the legends

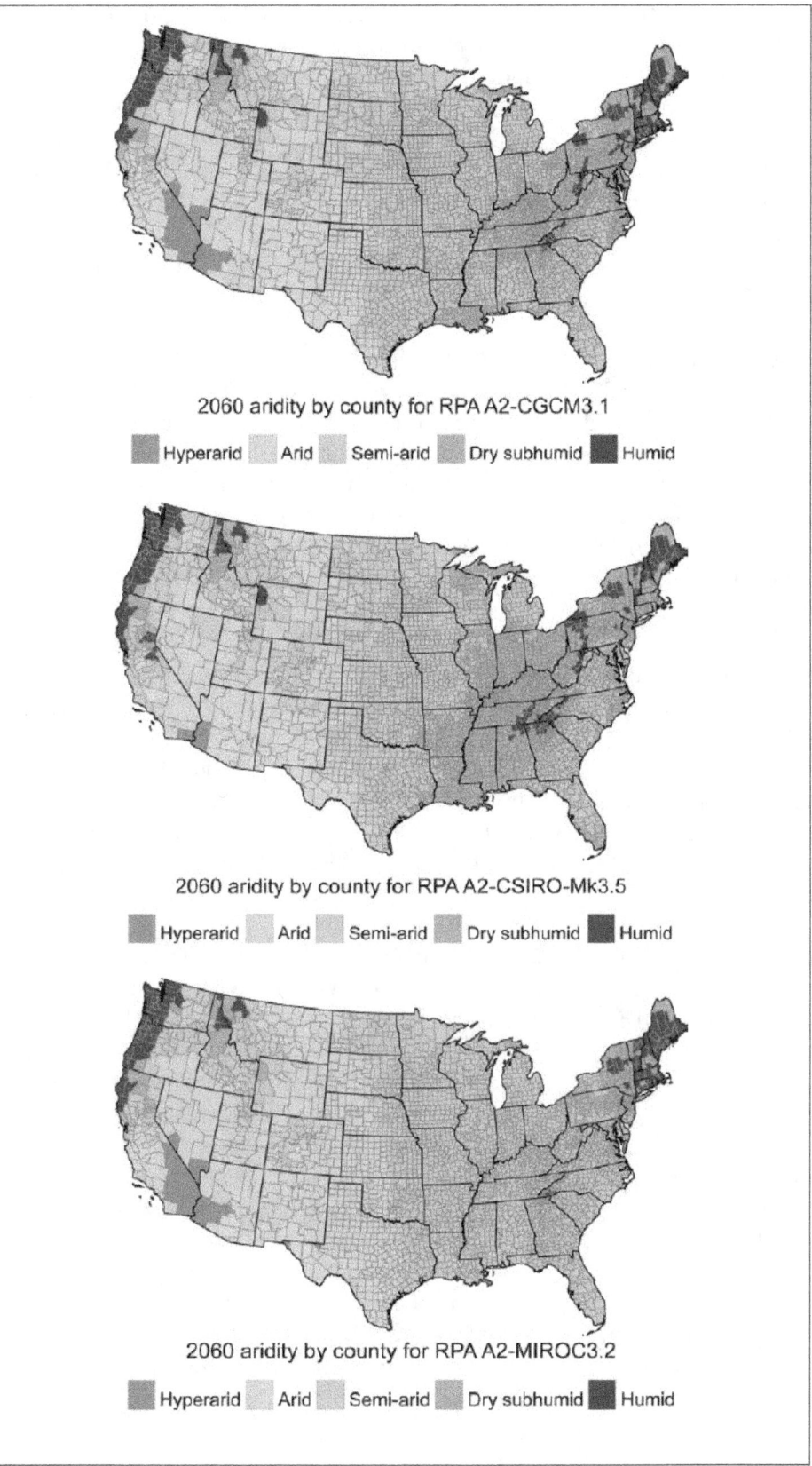

2060 aridity by county for RPA A2-CGCM3.1

Hyperarid   Arid   Semi-arid   Dry subhumid   Humid

2060 aridity by county for RPA A2-CSIRO-Mk3.5

Hyperarid   Arid   Semi-arid   Dry subhumid   Humid

2060 aridity by county for RPA A2-MIROC3.2

Hyperarid   Arid   Semi-arid   Dry subhumid   Humid

Figure 8.—2060 aridity by county for RPA A2-CGCM3.1, A2-CSIRO-Mk3.5, and A2-MIROC3.2

to be a 0.04 increase in the CGCM3.1 model. These changes do not change the aridity class of either state. Washington is projected to remain the least arid state in 2060 in all three models, but it is also becoming more arid with a range of increases from 0.20 in the CSIRO-Mk3.5 results to 0.12 in the CGCM3.1 projection. Despite this substantial increase, the aridity class for Washington does not change.

Imperial County, California, continues to be the most arid county in all three 2060 projections with an aridity ratio of 0.02 in the CSIRO-Mk3.5 results (no change from 2000) and a ratio of 0.01 (an aridity increase of 0.01) in the other two models (Fig. 8). The most humid county among all three models in 2060 continues to be Jefferson County, Washington, but its aridity increases from 2000, ranging from a change of 0.52 in the CSIRO-Mk3.5 and MIROC3.2 results to a 0.30 difference in the CGCM3.1 projection. None of the counties listed above change aridity class.

Like RPA scenario A1B, the frequency and magnitude of aridity increases are greater than decreases and variable across the United States (Fig. 9). In model CGCM3.1, the range of change is -0.03 to 0.58 with the greatest change (increase of aridity) found along the Pacific coast. The CSIRO-Mk3.5 projection has the greatest range of change: -0.07 to 0.67; but it has the greatest area of no change or a decrease in aridity, notably in the Southwest. Of note is the area of northwestern Texas that is projected to shift from arid to semi-arid. The MIROC3.2 model illustrates only increases in aridity, with a range of 0.01 to 0.60. The greatest change is found in the Pacific Northwest and in the South, especially along the southern Mississippi River basin.

The counties with the greatest projected increase of aridity are Tillamook County, Oregon, in both CGCM3.1 and MIROC3.2 models (changes of 0.58 and 0.60 respectively) and Skamania County, Washington (a change of 0.67) in the CSIRO-Mk3.5 projection. In both cases aridity class does not change. In the CGCM3.1 model, the county with the greatest

projected decrease in aridity is Big Horn County, Montana, with a change of -0.03. In addition, Big Horn County converts from an arid classification to a semi-arid classification. In the CSIRO-Mk3.5 projection, the greatest decrease in aridity is Tulare County, California, a change of -0.07, but it has no change in aridity class. In the MIROC3.2 model, the smallest increase of aridity is Imperial County, California, with an increase of 0.01 but no change in aridity class.

Scenario RPA B2

Across all three climate projections in RPA B2, aridity of the conterminous United States is projected to increase between 2000 and 2060. The projected aridity ratio (P/PE) in 2060 ranges from 0.38 (an increase of 0.11) from the CGCM2 model to 0.40 (an increase of 0.09) from the HADCM3 results (Table 5). The aridity class remains the same as 2000: semi-arid. The pattern of conversion in RPA scenario B2 is similar to the previous two scenarios with the CGCM2 model with the greatest change followed by CSIRO-Mk2 and HADCM3 projections.

In 2060, hyperarid land area of the conterminous United States is projected to increase in two models ranging from a 1.2 percent increase in the CSIRO-Mk2 projection to a 0.9 percent increase in the CGCM2 model (Table 6). In the HADCM3 results, there is a decrease in hyperarid land area of 0.2 percent from 2000. Arid land area increases in all three projections, ranging from a 9.2 percent rise in the HADCM3 results to a 5.2 percent increase in the CGCM2 model. Semi-arid land area increases in all three projections, ranging from a 17.7 percent increase with the CGCM2 projection to 7.6 percent growth in the HADCM3 results. Dry subhumid land decreases among all models, ranging from a 16.1 percent reduction in the CGCM2 results to an 8.3 percent reduction in the HADCM3 projection. Humid land area also decreases in the three projections, ranging from an 8.5 percent decline in the HADCM3 results to a 7.9 percent decrease in the CGCM2 model.

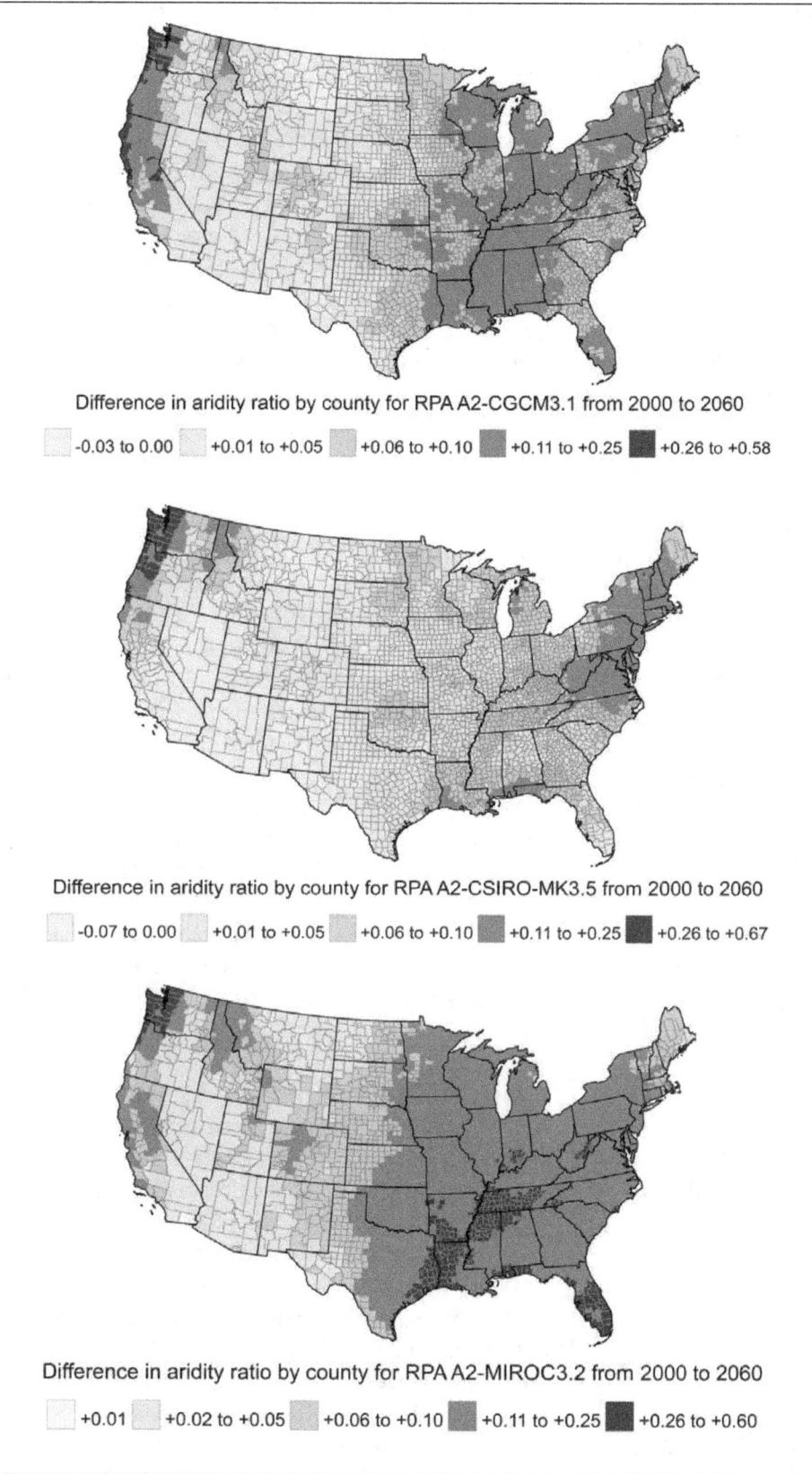

Difference in aridity ratio by county for RPA A2-CGCM3.1 from 2000 to 2060

-0.03 to 0.00   +0.01 to +0.05   +0.06 to +0.10   +0.11 to +0.25   +0.26 to +0.58

Difference in aridity ratio by county for RPA A2-CSIRO-MK3.5 from 2000 to 2060

-0.07 to 0.00   +0.01 to +0.05   +0.06 to +0.10   +0.11 to +0.25   +0.26 to +0.67

Difference in aridity ratio by county for RPA A2-MIROC3.2 from 2000 to 2060

+0.01   +0.02 to +0.05   +0.06 to +0.10   +0.11 to +0.25   +0.26 to +0.60

Figure 9.—Difference in aridity ratio by county for RPA A2-CGCM3.1, A2-CSIRO-Mk3.5, and A2-MIROC3.2 from 2000 to 2060. Maximum and minimum values are represented in the legends

In all three models, Arizona continues to be the most arid state. In the HADCM3 projection, Arizona does become slightly less arid, a 0.02 decrease, but otherwise the state becomes more arid, with a 0.01 increase in the CGCM2 projection results and a 0.02 increase in the CSIRO-Mk2 model. Arizona does not change aridity class. Washington is projected to continue as the least arid state in two models, but it has increasing aridity ranging from a 0.27 change in the CSIRO-Mk2 results to a 0.12 change in the CGCM2 model. Neither change affects Washington's aridity class. In the HADCM3 projection, Rhode Island is the least arid state but with increasing aridity of 0.09. The change has no effect on the aridity class for Rhode Island.

Imperial County, California, continues to be the most arid county projected in all three 2060 results with an aridity ratio of 0.02 in the CGCM2 and CSIRO-Mk2 results (no change from 2000) and a ratio of 0.04 (a decrease of aridity of 0.02, but no change in aridity class) in the HADCM3 model (Fig. 10). The least arid county among all three models in 2060 continues to be Jefferson County, Washington, but its aridity is projected to increase from 2000, ranging from a change of 1.21 in the HADCM3 results to a 0.24 difference in the CGCM2 projection. Neither change affects the county aridity class.

Like the previous two RPA scenarios, the frequency and magnitude of increasing aridity are greater than the decreases and variable across the United States (Fig. 11). The range of change in model CGCM2 is -0.03 to 0.49, and the greatest projected changes are located in the Pacific Northwest and in the Appalachian Mountains. In projection CSIRO-Mk2 the range of change is -0.02 to 0.95 with the greatest change found along the northern Pacific Coast from northern California to Washington. The greatest range of change is found in the HADCM3 results: -0.05 to 1.21. Like the previous model, the greatest projected aridity increase is found along the northern Pacific coast.

The counties with the greatest increase of aridity are Tillamook County, Oregon, in both CGCM2 and CSIRO-Mk2 models (changes of 0.49 and 0.95

respectively), and Jefferson County, Washington (a change of 1.21), in the HADCM3 projection. The changes in aridity ratio do not affect the aridity class in either county. In the CGCM2 model, the county with the greatest projected decrease in aridity is Calhoun County, Texas, with a change of -0.03. The change in ratio does not affect aridity class. In the CSIRO-Mk2 projection, the greatest increase of humidity is Butte County, Idaho, a change of -0.02 with no effect on county aridity class. In the HADCM3 results, the largest decrease of aridity is Yavapai County, Arizona, with a difference of 0.05. The change in ratio does not affect the county aridity class.

Aridity Discussion

In all nine scenarios, the aridity of the conterminous United States is projected to increase by 2060, ranging from an increase of 0.05 (from 0.49 in 2000 to 0.44 in 2060) in RPA A1B-CGCM 3.1 and RPA A2-CSIRO-Mk3.5 to an increase of 0.19 (from 0.49 in 2000 to 0.30 in 2060) in RPA A1B-MIROC3.2 (Table 5). Despite these changes, the aridity class for the United States does not change—it remains semi-arid for all projections. Among the three climate model sets across the conterminous United States, the most arid projections come from the MIROC3.2 (A1B and A2) and HADCM3 (B2) models with an average aridity in 2060 of 0.24 (with the two MIROC3.2 scenarios substantially more arid than the HADCM3), followed by the CGCM model set (0.31), and CSIRO model set (0.32). Among the three RPA scenarios, RPA A1B is the most arid (2060 aridity at 0.38), followed by RPA A2 and B2, each at 0.39.

Changes in the amount of hyperarid areas (0.5 percent of the conterminous United States in 2000) range from a 2.0 percent increase in RPA A1B-MIROC 3.2 and RPA A2-MIROC 3.2 to a decrease of 0.2 percent in 2060 in RPA B2-HADCM3 (Table 6, Fig. 12). For arid regions (26.3 of the conterminous United States in 2000), the projection varies from a 12.7 percent increase in 2060 RPA A1B-MIROC3.2 to a decrease of 0.7 percent in 2060 RPA A2-CSIRO-Mk3.5. Semi-arid areas (35.3 percent in 2000) are projected to increase by 6.2 percent in 2060 RPA A1B-CSIRO-Mk3.5 to as much as a 17.7 percent in 2060 RPA B2-CGCM2. Dry subhumid areas (25.2 percent in 2000) are projected

2060 aridity by county for RPA B2-CGCM2

Hyperarid   Arid   Semi-arid   Dry subhumid   Humid

2060 aridity by county for RPA B2-CSIRO-Mk2

Hyperarid   Arid   Semi-arid   Dry subhumid   Humid

2060 aridity by county for RPA B2-HADCM3

Hyperarid   Arid   Semi-arid   Dry subhumid   Humid

Figure 10.—2060 aridity by county for RPA B2-CGCM2, B2-CSIRO-Mk2, and B2-HADCM3

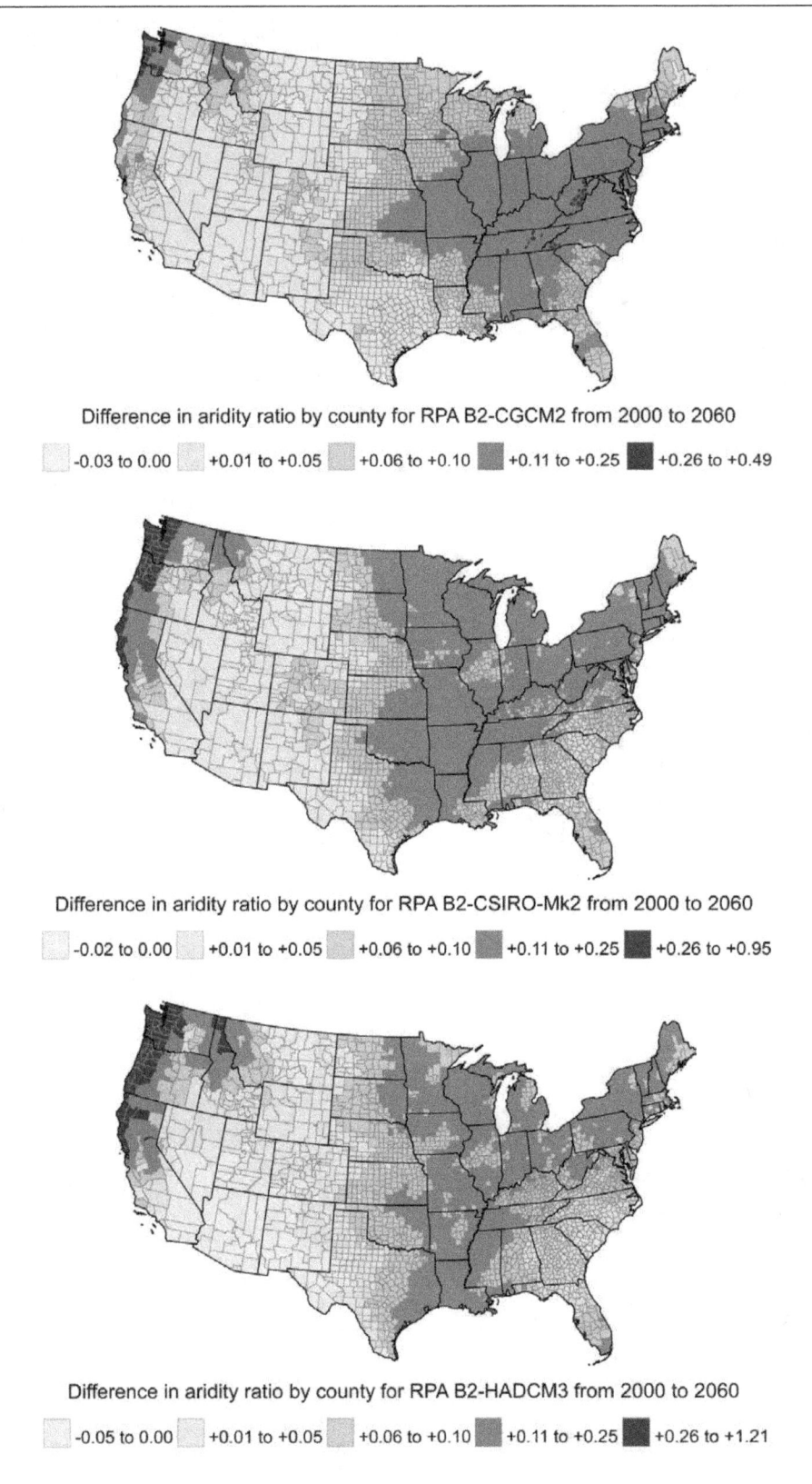

Difference in aridity ratio by county for RPA B2-CGCM2 from 2000 to 2060

-0.03 to 0.00   +0.01 to +0.05   +0.06 to +0.10   +0.11 to +0.25   +0.26 to +0.49

Difference in aridity ratio by county for RPA B2-CSIRO-Mk2 from 2000 to 2060

-0.02 to 0.00   +0.01 to +0.05   +0.06 to +0.10   +0.11 to +0.25   +0.26 to +0.95

Difference in aridity ratio by county for RPA B2-HADCM3 from 2000 to 2060

-0.05 to 0.00   +0.01 to +0.05   +0.06 to +0.10   +0.11 to +0.25   +0.26 to +1.21

Figure 11.—Difference in aridity ratio by county for RPA B2-CGCM2, B2-CSIRO-Mk2, and B2-HADCM3 from 2000 to 2060. Maximum and minimum values are represented in the legends

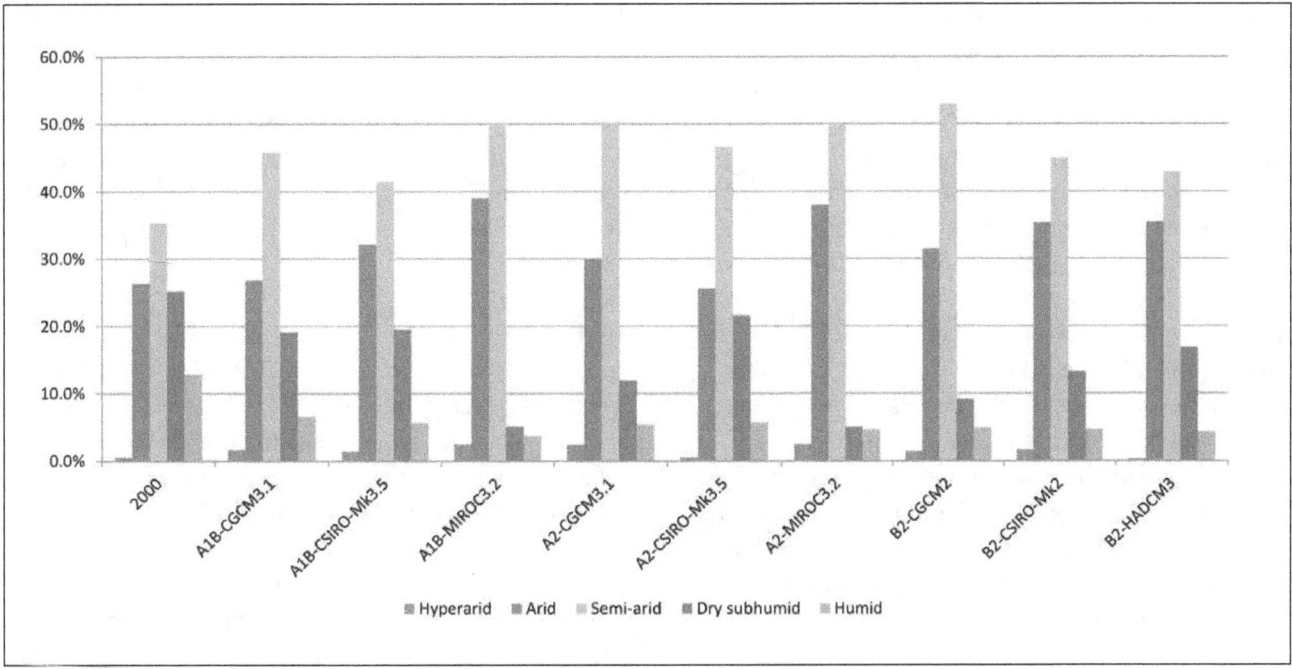

Figure 12.—Distribution of categories of aridity for the conterminous United States from 2000 to 2060 across all nine climate change projections

to decrease by as much as 20.2 percent in 2060 RPA A2-MIROC3.2 to as little as 3.6 percent in 2060 RPA A2-CSIRO-Mk3.5. Humid areas (12.8 percent in 2000) are also projected to decrease with the greatest decrease of 9.1 percent in 2060 RPA A1B-MIROC3.2 and the smallest decrease of 6.2 percent in 2060 RPA A1B-CGCM3.1.

The frequency and magnitude of increasing aridity across the conterminous United States is greater than decreases in aridity. While the patterns vary among the nine scenario-climate combinations, the greatest changes exist among the areas classified as dry subhumid and humid in 2000. For the most part, substantial increases in aridity occur along the northern Pacific coast of northern California through Washington, and from the Great Plains states to the South Central and Southeastern states, and to the Northeast states. As previously illustrated, the general trend is a conversion of areas of dry subhumid to areas categorized as semi-arid.

Overall, the aridity change for the entire conterminous United States is not large, but this analysis illustrates the variability of aridity changes at the county scale and demonstrates that some areas, like the counties of the northern Pacific Coast, may have larger increases in aridity and greater potential impacts to those ecosystems. As reported by the RPA Assessment (U.S. Forest Service 2012a), climate change will impact ecosystems and their derived benefits, and ecosystems will have diverse responses to stress caused by climate change. In particular, the assessment emphasizes that climate change may have greater influence on fragile ecosystems and ecosystems found in the transition zones between major biomes, like the grassland-forest land transition in the central United States and areas of high topographic relief, like those found in the Intermountain west. These influences can cause habitat stress and ecosystem change that may result in decreased capacity for sustained regeneration, species decline, and species mix changes, such as the projected general decline of lodgepole pine and

Douglas fir throughout the Rocky Mountains, or the decline of hemlock-Sitka spruce along the northern Pacific coast, which has some of the greatest increases in aridity. Climate change can also lead to increased stress in ecosystems making them more susceptible to invasive species and wildfire, such as the increased threat of bark beetle infestation and wildfire in the western states (U.S. Forest Service 2012a).

The RPA Assessment (U.S. Forest Service 2012a) projects that climate change will increase the areas vulnerable to water shortage because of decreasing tree cover, decreased precipitation, and increased demand for water resources. The most vulnerable area of overlapping increased aridity and increased water shortage vulnerability is the agricultural center of the conterminous United States just west of the Mississippi River.

Throughout the conterminous United States, the ability to sustain tree cover and related species mix may be compromised by climate change and increasing aridity. Tree cover loss from land use change may further impact those ecosystems stressed by climate change. The next section examines the regions of the conterminous United States that may be at risk by both increasing aridity and land use derived tree cover loss.

Aridity and Tree Cover Change Index Scenario: RPA A1B

In the 2000 to 2060 aridity and tree cover change index for RPA scenario A1B-CGCM3.1 (Fig. 13), the greatest projected impact from tree cover loss and/or increasing aridity is found along the Pacific Coast, urbanizing counties, developing counties on the edges of protected lands, and highlands east of the Mississippi River. Many of these regions were within humid, dry subhumid and semi-arid areas and had a relatively high percent tree cover in 2000. Five of the bottom 10 counties with the lowest index scores are in the Pacific Northwest near the coast, which have high tree cover and low aridity. Generally, the areas demonstrating positive values of the change index are in low tree cover areas in the arid and semi-arid regions of the Intermountain and Great Plains states, including most of Nebraska. Much of

the Southwest has little change. Dare County, North Carolina, is projected to have the greatest impact from both increased aridity and/or decreased tree cover. In Dare County, the aridity increases 0.04, and percent tree cover decreases 44.2 percent. Lincoln County, Washington, has the greatest index value with aridity increasing 0.02 and tree cover percent increasing 9.2 percent.

In the 2000 to 2060 aridity and tree cover change index for RPA scenario A1B-CSIRO-Mk3.5, the greatest impact from projected tree cover loss and/or increasing aridity is similar to the pattern from the CGCM3.1 model above, with expanded impacts in the Midwest, and less severity overall. Like CGCM3.1, the lowest index scores are found in the Pacific Northwest. The areas demonstrating minor positive values of the change index are in more sparsely-treed areas in the arid and semi-arid counties of west Texas, Nebraska, and scattered throughout the Intermountain states. The exception is Florida and South Carolina where tree cover is moderate and where the aridity is mostly in the dry subhumid category. The region of little or no change covers of the remainder of the Great Plains and Intermountain region. Snohomish County, Washington, has the greatest impact from both increased aridity and decreased percent tree cover. In Snohomish County, the aridity increases 0.58, and tree cover decreases 11.3 percent. Lincoln County, Idaho, has the most positive value with aridity increasing 0.01 and tree cover increasing 7.2 percent.

In the 2000 to 2060 aridity and tree cover change index for RPA scenario A1B-MIROC3.2, the greatest impact from tree cover loss and/or increasing aridity is found in most of the states east of the Great Plains, and like the previous patterns, also in the Pacific Northwest and scattered urbanizing and developing counties. This climate model has the broadest impact of the three models in the RPA A1B scenario. Five of the ten lowest index scores are found in Georgia with most of those five in the Atlanta region. There are very few counties with positive index scores found in Idaho and eastern Washington. The areas with little to no change are found scattered throughout the Intermountain region. Dare County, North Carolina,

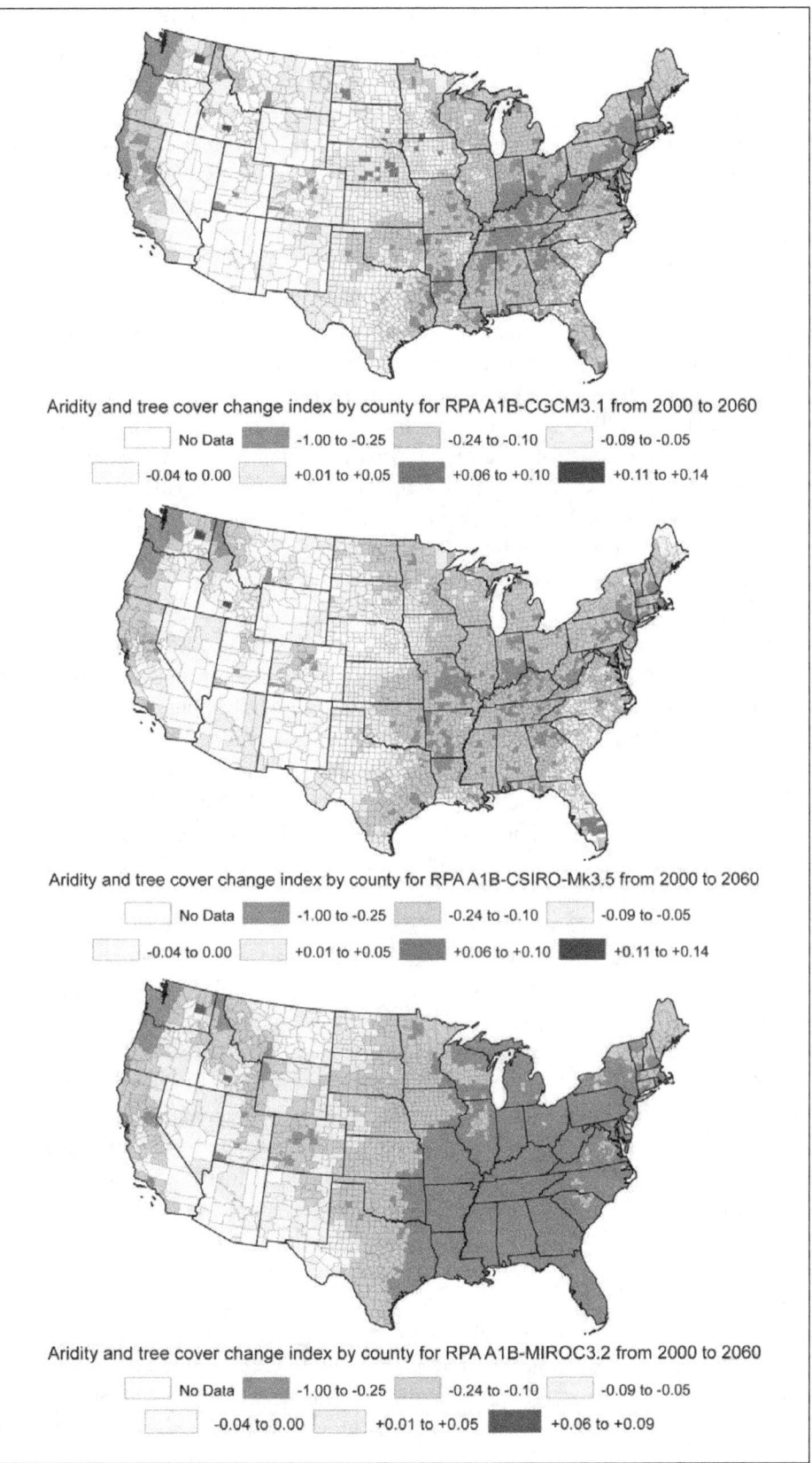

Aridity and tree cover change index by county for RPA A1B-CGCM3.1 from 2000 to 2060

No Data   -1.00 to -0.25   -0.24 to -0.10   -0.09 to -0.05

-0.04 to 0.00   +0.01 to +0.05   +0.06 to +0.10   +0.11 to +0.14

Aridity and tree cover change index by county for RPA A1B-CSIRO-Mk3.5 from 2000 to 2060

No Data   -1.00 to -0.25   -0.24 to -0.10   -0.09 to -0.05

-0.04 to 0.00   +0.01 to +0.05   +0.06 to +0.10   +0.11 to +0.14

Aridity and tree cover change index by county for RPA A1B-MIROC3.2 from 2000 to 2060

No Data   -1.00 to -0.25   -0.24 to -0.10   -0.09 to -0.05

-0.04 to 0.00   +0.01 to +0.05   +0.06 to +0.09

Figure 13.—Aridity and tree cover change index for RPA A1B-CGCM3.1, A1B-CSIRO-Mk3.5, and A1B-MIROC3.2 from 2000 to 2060

has the greatest impact from both increased aridity and decreased percent tree cover. In Dare County, the aridity increases 0.21, and tree cover decreases 44.2 percent. Lincoln County, Washington, has the most positive index value with aridity increasing 0.05 and tree cover increasing 9.2 percent.

Scenario: RPA A2

In the 2000 to 2060 aridity and tree cover change index for RPA scenario A2-CGCM3.1 (Fig. 14), the greatest impact from tree cover loss and/or increasing aridity is found in the Pacific Coast States and in urbanizing counties, developing counties on the edges of protected lands scattered throughout the states of the east, with heavier concentrations in the South. Many of these regions were within humid, dry subhumid and semi-arid areas and had high tree cover in 2000. The counties with the lowest index scores are in the Pacific Northwest, Georgia, Virginia, California, Florida, and North Carolina. Generally, the regions with positive index values are found in the northern Intermountain (much of eastern Montana), Great Plains states, and in west Texas, areas categorized as arid and semi-arid and with low tree cover. Little or no change occurs in scattered counties among the Intermountain and Great Plains states. Dare County, North Carolina, has the greatest projected impact from both increased aridity and decreased percent tree cover. In Dare County, the aridity increases 0.08, and tree cover decreases 44.2 percent. Val Verde County, Texas, has the most positive index value with aridity increasing 0.04 and tree cover increasing 15.1 percent.

In the 2000 to 2060 aridity and tree cover change index for RPA scenario A2-CSIRO-Mk3.5, the greatest impact from tree cover loss and/or increasing aridity is found in the Pacific Northwest states, Northeastern states, scattered throughout the Southeast, and in urbanizing and developing counties, similar to the patterns previously described. Most of the counties with the 10 lowest index scores are found in the Pacific Northwest. Generally, the regions with positive index values are found in the Southwest region extending from west Texas to California, to the north through the Intermountain states, and within Nebraska, Iowa, Illinois, and Kansas. The areas of

little to no change are found throughout the center of the conterminous United States. Dare County, North Carolina, has the greatest impact from both increased aridity and decreased percent tree cover. In Dare County, the aridity increases 0.09, and tree cover decreases 44.2 percent. Val Verde County, Texas, has the most positive value with aridity increasing 0.02 and tree cover increasing 15.1 percent.

In the 2000 to 2060 aridity and tree cover change index for RPA scenario A2-MIROC3.2, the greatest projected impact from tree cover loss and/or increasing aridity is found in the Pacific Northwest states, in a region extending from the Midwest and east Texas to the Atlantic coast, and within the urbanizing and developing counties, similar to the patterns found in the previous models. The pattern of counties with the lowest index scores is similar to those described from the A2-CGCM3.1 model above. Only a few counties have positive index values found in Washington, Idaho, and Texas. Little or no change is found scattered throughout the Intermountain states. Dare County, North Carolina, has the greatest impact from both increased aridity and decreased percent tree cover. In Dare County, the aridity increases 0.18, and tree cover decreases 44.2 percent. Val Verde County, Texas, has the most positive value with aridity increasing 0.09 and tree cover increasing 15.1 percent.

Scenario: RPA B2

In the 2000 to 2060 aridity and tree cover change index for RPA scenario B2-CGCM2 (Fig. 15), the greatest impact from tree cover loss and/or increasing aridity is found in the Pacific Northwest states, urbanizing counties, developing counties on the edges of protected lands, and in a region extending from Missouri to the east through the Midwest and South Central states to the Mid-Atlantic. Many of these regions were within humid, dry subhumid and semi-arid areas and had high tree cover in 2000. Most of the counties with the lowest 10 index scores are in the Pacific Northwest and in the Atlanta, Georgia, metropolitan region. Positive index values are scattered throughout the Intermountain region and in southeast coastal Texas. Little or no change in index values are found in Texas and through the

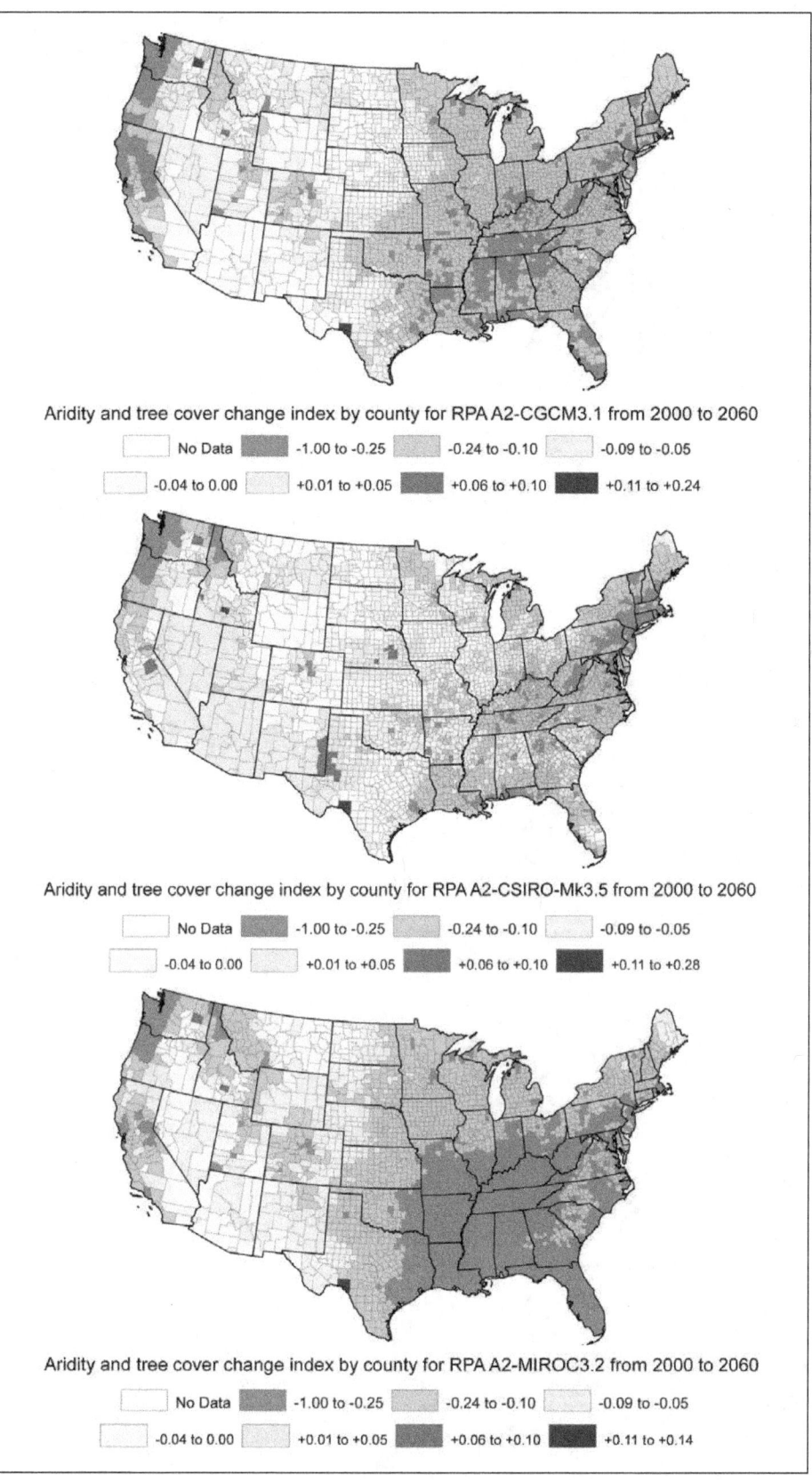

Aridity and tree cover change index by county for RPA A2-CGCM3.1 from 2000 to 2060

| No Data | -1.00 to -0.25 | -0.24 to -0.10 | -0.09 to -0.05 |
| -0.04 to 0.00 | +0.01 to +0.05 | +0.06 to +0.10 | +0.11 to +0.24 |

Aridity and tree cover change index by county for RPA A2-CSIRO-Mk3.5 from 2000 to 2060

| No Data | -1.00 to -0.25 | -0.24 to -0.10 | -0.09 to -0.05 |
| -0.04 to 0.00 | +0.01 to +0.05 | +0.06 to +0.10 | +0.11 to +0.28 |

Aridity and tree cover change index by county for RPA A2-MIROC3.2 from 2000 to 2060

| No Data | -1.00 to -0.25 | -0.24 to -0.10 | -0.09 to -0.05 |
| -0.04 to 0.00 | +0.01 to +0.05 | +0.06 to +0.10 | +0.11 to +0.14 |

Figure 14.—Aridity and tree cover change index for RPA A2-CGCM3.1, A2-CSIRO-Mk3.5, and A2-MIROC3.2 from 2000 to 2060

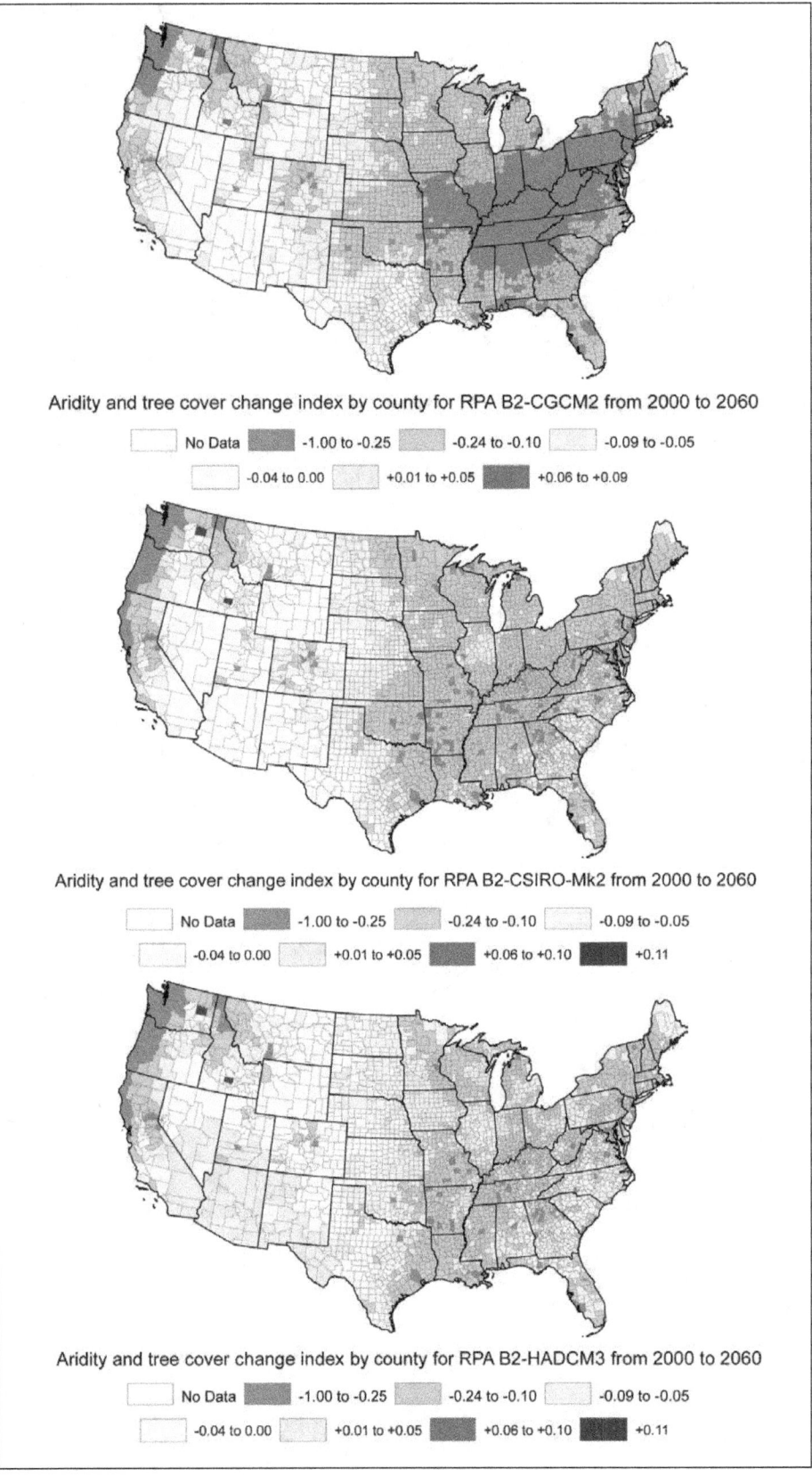

Figure 15.—Aridity and tree cover change index for RPA B2-CGCM2, B2-CSIRO-Mk2, and B2-HADCM3 from 2000 to 2060

Intermountain states. Dare County, North Carolina, has the greatest impact from both increased aridity and decreased percent tree cover. In Dare County, the aridity increases 0.12 and tree cover decreases 44.2 percent. Lincoln County, Washington, has the most positive value with aridity increasing 0.04 and tree cover increasing 8.1 percent.

In the 2000 to 2060 climate and tree cover change index for RPA scenario B2-CSIRO-Mk2, the greatest projected impact from tree cover loss and/or increasing aridity is found along the Pacific Coast and scattered throughout the conterminous United States, but with less severity than the B2-CGCM2 scenario. Most of the counties with the lowest index scores are found in the Pacific Northwest. The counties with positive index values are found mostly in Idaho, areas that generally had low tree cover and that were more arid in 2000. The area of little or no change is found in the Intermountain and Great Plains states. Dare County, North Carolina, has the greatest impact from both increased aridity and decreased percent tree cover. In Dare County, the aridity increases 0.07, and tree cover decreases 44.2 percent. Lincoln County, Idaho, has the most positive value with aridity increasing 0.01 and tree cover increasing 8.1 percent.

In the 2000 to 2060 climate and tree cover change index for RPA scenario B2-HADCM3, the greatest projected impact from tree cover loss and/or increasing aridity is found along the Pacific Coast and with a very similar pattern to the previous scenario. Most of the counties with the lowest 10 index scores are in the Pacific Northwest. The regions with positive index values are found in the Southwest, including most of Arizona. The area of little or no change is found in a pattern similar to the previous scenario. Dare County, North Carolina, has the greatest impact from both increased aridity and decreased percent tree cover. In Dare County, the aridity increases 0.05, and tree cover decreases 44.2 percent. Lincoln County, Washington, has the most positive value on the other side of the spectrum with aridity increasing 0.09 and tree cover increasing 8.1 percent.

Discussion

When the aridity and tree cover projections are combined across the conterminous United States, the scenario with the least tree cover loss and smallest increase in aridity is 2060 RPA B2-HADCM3. The scenario with the greatest percent tree cover loss and greatest increase in aridity in 2060 is RPA A1B-MIROC3.2. Consistent among all scenarios is that the tree cover losses and aridity increases, illustrated by the combination of both indicators, are of greater frequency and magnitude throughout most of the conterminous United States. The regions of the greatest impact from both increased aridity and/or decreased tree cover are relatively consistent among the scenarios with counties of the Pacific Northwest and Southeast having some of the lowest index scores. In addition, scattered urbanizing and developing counties, including some that border protected lands also tend to have low index scores. The Southwest and Intermountain regions are generally areas of little or no aridity increase and/or tree cover increase among all scenarios. The areas of greatest change tend to be the least arid regions with high tree cover. Much of this same area overlaps regions of established and expanding human settlement, such as the growing metropolitan region in the Pacific Northwest states (between the Cascade and Coast Ranges), and around Atlanta, Georgia. Human population growth, urbanization, and low density development is the primary driver of tree cover loss, and while increasing aridity may not be caused by local impacts of human expansion, many of the same areas of the lowest aridity and impacted by aridity increases are also areas of established and expanding human settlement.

As summarized in the previous sections of tree cover and aridity changes, tree cover loss will decrease forest inventories and carbon stocks, degrade habitat, and impact water availability while the demands for the goods and services from ecosystems increase. Aridity increases will also impact ecosystems and cause diverse ecosystem responses to the stress caused by climate change. Those changes could be particularly acute in more sensitive ecosystems. Ultimately, the combination of tree loss and aridity increase could impair the stability of existing ecosystems and their ongoing sustainability. The stress to these systems could lead to impaired regeneration, species decline, species mix change, and increase the vulnerability to other threats such as invasive species and wildfire. Finally, increasing aridity will increase water supply vulnerability, and many of the areas projected to gain tree cover may not increase in cover because of increasing demands on a shrinking water supply.

Future development and climate change will have significant and varying effects on tree cover and ecosystems in the United States with most areas projected to lose tree cover and become more arid by 2060. Aridity is projected to increase because of continued global climate change. Both decreases and increases of tree cover are driven by human population growth, urbanization, and low density development, with decreases in tree cover found in the forested areas and increases in tree cover in sparsely treed land uses that convert to developed land uses. These developed land uses tend to remove trees in forest regions and bring in trees and increase tree cover in low tree cover regions. Thus, the tree and forest landscape of the United States are likely to undergo substantial changes in the coming century. Managers and planners need to understand these changes to help sustain healthy and functioning landscapes to meet the needs of changing society.

⬚⬚⬚⬚⬚⬚S⬚⬚

This report provides further detail in support of the 2010 RPA Assessment by illustrating the variability of tree cover and aridity changes throughout the conterminous United States. We found that in all projections that the conterminous United States loses tree cover in 2060, ranging from 1.1 to 1.6 percent; and that the conterminous United States is becoming more arid in 2060, ranging from a 0.05 to a 0.19 increase in aridity ratio. Overall, the frequency and magnitude of percent tree cover losses and aridity increases among the counties of the conterminous United States are greater than percent tree cover gains and decreases in aridity. Mapping these areas of change illustrates the areas at greatest risk of ecological change from tree loss and increased aridity.

These higher risk areas are generally in rapidly urbanizing regions with high tree cover and low aridity, such as those found in the metropolitan regions of the Pacific Northwest, Southeast, and Northeast. Despite this generalization, tree cover and aridity change is highly variable throughout the conterminous United States.

Land development will continue to threaten the integrity of natural ecosystems driven by projected population growth, urbanization, and low density development including agricultural uses at the expense of natural landscapes. This development will cause natural habitat loss, but also increase the amount of urban land in the United States. Trees and forests in urban areas will become increasingly important in providing benefits to both humans and nature. Climate change will alter natural ecosystems and affect their ability to provide goods and services. In particular aridity changes may have a greater impact on more sensitive and vulnerable ecosystems. As population increases and natural land cover decreases, the competition for goods and services from natural ecosystems will increase, especially at the wildland-urban interface. The impacts are geographically variable, and resource responses to land development and climate change drivers will require national, regional, and local strategies to address future resource management issues.

⬚T⬚RAT⬚R⬚ ⬚T⬚D

Coulson, D.P.; Joyce, L.A. 2010. **Historical climate data (1940-2006) for the conterminous United States at the county spatial scale based on PRISM climatology.** Fort Collins, CO: U.S. Department of Agriculture, Forest Service, Rocky Mountain Research Station. http://dx.doi.org/10.2737/RDS-2010-0010

Coulson, D.P.; Joyce, L.A.; Price, D.T.; McKenney, D.W. 2010a. **Climate scenarios for the conterminous United States at the county spatial scale using SRES scenario B2 and PRISM climatology.** Fort Collins, CO: U.S. Department of Agriculture, Forest Service, Rocky Mountain Research Station. http://dx.doi.org/10.2737/RDS-2010-0009

Coulson, D.P.; Joyce, L.A.; Price, D.T.; McKenney, D.W.; Siltanen, R.M.; Papadopol, P.; Lawrence, K. 2010b. **Climate scenarios for the conterminous United States at the county spatial scale using SRES scenarios A1B and A2 and PRISM climatology.** Fort Collins, CO: U.S. Department of Agriculture, Forest Service, Rocky Mountain Research Station. http://dx.doi.org/10.2737/RDS-2010-0008

Forest and Rangeland Renewable Resources Planning Act of 1974 [RPA]; 16 U.S.C. 1601 (note).

Hardy, S.D.; Koontz, T.M. 2010. **Collaborative watershed partnerships in urban and rural areas: Different pathways to success?** Landscape and Urban Planning. 95(3): 79-90.

Intergovernmental Panel on Climate Change [IPCC]. 2007. **Climate Change 2007: Synthesis report.** Contribution of Working Groups I, II and III to the Fourth Assessment. Geneva, Switzerland: Intergovernmental Panel on Climate Change. 104 p.

Joyce, L.A.; Price, D.T.; Coulson, D.P. [et al.]. [In review]. **Projecting climate change in the United States: a technical document supporting the Forest Service 2010 RPA Assessment.** Gen. Tech. Rep. RMRS. Fort Collins, CO: U.S. Department of Agriculture, Forest Service, Rocky Mountain Research Station.

Kuo, F.E.; Sullivan, W.E. 2001. **Environment and crime in the inner city: does vegetation reduce crime?** Environmental Behavior. 33(3): 343-365.

Middleton, N.; Thomas, D., eds. 1997. **World atlas of desertification 2nd ed.** London, UK: Routledge. 192 p.

Nakicenovic, N.; Swart, R., eds. 2000. **Special report on emissions scenarios.** Prepared for the Intergovernmental Panel on Climate Change. Cambridge, UK: Cambridge University Press. 570 p. Available: http://www.ipcc.ch/ipccreports/sres/emission/index.htm.

Nowak, D.J.; Dwyer, J.F. 2007. **Understanding the benefits and costs of urban forest ecosystems.** In: Kuser, J., ed. Urban and community forestry in the northeast. New York, NY: Springer: 25-46.

Nowak, D.J.; Greenfield, E.J. 2010. **Evaluating the national land cover database tree cover and impervious cover estimates across the conterminous United States: a comparison with photo-interpreted estimates.** Environmental Management. 46(3): 378-390.

Ostrom, E. 1990. **Governing the commons: the evolution of institutions for collective actions.** Cambridge, UK: Cambridge University Press. 298 p.

Wear, D.N. 2011. **Forecasts of county-level land uses under three future scenarios: A technical document supporting the Forest Service 2010 RPA Assessment.** Gen. Tech. Rep. SRS-141. Asheville, NC: U.S. Department of Agriculture Forest Service, Southern Research Station. 41 p.

Westphal, L.M. 2003. **Urban greening and social benefits: a study of empowerment outcomes.** Journal of Arboriculture. 29(3): 137-147.

Wolf, K.M. 2003. **Public response to the urban forest in inner-city business districts.** Journal of Arboriculture. 29(3): 117-126.

Ulrich, R.S. 1984. **View through a window may influence recovery from surgery.** Science. 224: 420-421.

U.S. Forest Service. 2012a. **Future of America's forests and rangelands: Forest Service 2010 Resources Planning Act Assessment.** Gen. Tech. Rept. WO-87. Washington, DC: U.S. Department of Agriculture, Forest Service, Washington Office. 198 p.

U.S. Forest Service. 2012b. **Future scenarios: a technical document supporting the Forest Service 2010 RPA Assessment.** Gen. Tech. Rep. RMRS-272. Fort Collins, CO: U.S. Department of Agriculture, Forest Service, Rocky Mountain Research Station. 34 p.

U.S. Geologic Survey [USGS]. 2008. **Multi-resolution land characteristics consortium.** Washington, DC: U.S. Department of Interior, Geologic Survey. www.mrlc.gov. (2008 August 1).

Greenfield, Eric J.; Nowak, David J. 2013. **Tree cover and aridity projections to 2060: a technical document supporting the Forest Service 2010 RPA assessment.** Gen. Tech. Rep. NRS-125. Newtown Square, PA: U.S. Department of Agriculture, Forest Service, Northern Research Station. 35 p.

Future projections of tree cover and climate change are useful to natural resource managers as they illustrate potential changes to our natural resources and the ecosystem services they provide. This report a) details three projections of tree cover change across the conterminous United States based on predicted land-use changes from 2000 to 2060; b) evaluates nine climate projections for the same period to assess which areas of the country may become more or less arid; and c) provides an index of combined tree-cover and aridity change for nine modeled projections to illustrate which areas of the U.S. are projected to experience the greatest impact from tree-cover loss and increasing aridity. The index illustrates a new approach to highlight areas of ecological vulnerability or concern that may develop at the nexus of projected land use and climate change. We found that in all projections the conterminous U.S. loses tree cover by 2060, ranging from a 1.1 to 1.6 percent decline; and that the conterminous United States is becoming more arid by 2060, ranging from a 0.05 to 0.19 decrease in the aridity ratio. Overall, the frequency and magnitude of percent tree cover losses and aridity increases among the counties of the conterminous U.S. are greater than percent tree cover gains and decreases in aridity. The index illustrates that the areas at greatest risk of ecological change from tree loss and increased aridity generally are rapidly urbanizing regions of high tree cover and low aridity such as those found in the metropolitan regions of the Pacific Northwest, Southeast, and Northeast.

KEY WORDS: forecasting, land use change, climate change

Printed on recycled paper

USDA

United States Department of Agriculture

Forest Service

RPA

Northern Research Station

General Technical Report NRS-125

October 2013